*L*ife *& Death*

The Sages Speak About

Other Chinmaya Publication Series:

THE *Mananam* SERIES

The Sages Speak About
*L*ife & *Death*

CHINMAYA PUBLICATIONS

Chinmaya Publications
Main Office
P.O. Box 129
Piercy, CA 95587, USA

Chinmaya Publications
Distribution Office
560 Bridgetowne Pike
Langhorne, PA 19053, USA

Credits:

Series Editor: Margaret Leuverink
Front cover and text photographs: Gail Larrick

Library of Congress Catalog Card Number 94-93931

ISBN 1-880687-07-0

Contents

Preface

The topic of death, which still strikes fear in the heart of many, is coming out of its darkness, and being looked upon in a wondrous new light. This is due mainly to the research done by those dynamic men and women working in the ever-expanding field of psychology today. The subjective scientists, the sages, have always appreciated the fact that the processes of life and death go together, and that fear of death is ignorance of life itself. They knew that "life is a university to educate the soul," and tried to awaken everyone to this fact. But many of us discover the purpose of life only when there is very little life left. One can just imagine the regrets in the final hours, "Oh, if only, if only I had known that death was coming, I would have lived my life differently." Yet we all know that we are standing in the queue. No one even has the decency to come and ask us, "Hey, are you ready? It's your turn." The greatest wonder, as the rishis said thousands of years ago, is the fact that death is part of life and yet most of us do not even want to think about it.

Tzu Lu, a disciple of Confucius, once asked his Master about serving spiritual beings. Confucius said, "If we are not yet able to serve man, how can we serve spiritual beings?" Then Tzu Lu asked, "What about death?" Confucius said, "If we do not yet know about life, how can we know about death?"

The authors in this book are sages and spiritual teachers who are restating age-old truths in contemporary terms. They also urge us to give sufficient attention to life itself. They encourage us to use this precious gift of life in pursuing the ultimate goal and fulfillment of human life, which is to know ourselves at the core of our being.

We know instinctively that we are deathless and timeless beings, but because we have not yet touched upon this core, this ever-present Reality in us, we imagine ourselves as separate individuals. This feeling of separateness, also called ego, identifying itself with the body, naturally fears its extinction. To keep that fear from staying around too long, however, we busy ourselves with all kinds of things. But one day when confronted with the death of a loved one or a life-threatening illness, some of us may pause long enough to ask ourselves, "What is life? What is death? Is there something after death?"

The authors in Part One, "Death: A Process of Life," make a brave attempt to add to our understanding of death. They point out that without this understanding we are not able to live our lives fully. We learn that the fear of death is behind all our fears and that life can be lived fully and dynamically only when we understand its purpose. When we begin to think of death not as something final, but as a change in the condition of the body only, we gradually lose our fear of it. This becomes the topic of Part Two, "Overcoming the Fear of Death." The authors show that our present life, well-lived, brings fearlessness and joy and gives us power over the life to come.

Before we visit a foreign country, most of us study the customs and habits of the people that we will be visiting; some of us even take language courses so that we can communicate more effectively with our hosts. In the same way, in our journey to the world called death, some preparation is necessary. One could say, "How can we possibly prepare for something that we do not know?" But wait, we do know something about death. We know for certain that we have to leave behind not only our physical body, but also all the things and beings that we have become attached to. If the mind and intellect continue beyond the threshold of death, then it is they that need to grow in beauty. With a beautiful mind we will get a welcome reception, no matter where we go, even in the world beyond. Beautification or puri-fication of the mind also prepares us for its transcendence, not in another place or time, but right here and now.

Hence, the emphasis in Part Three, "Teachings for Life and Death," is on spiritual living. The only way to come out of the cycle of births and deaths is to attain spiritual knowledge. All the major religions assure us that the soul continues and that we are infinitely more than the body. Every one of the inspirational essays contained in this issue confirms this. We are encouraged to make spiritual pursuit the highest priority in our lives, for we never know when our hour will come.

M.L.

PART ONE

Death:
A Process of Life

If you would indeed
behold the spirit of death,
open your heart wide
unto the body of life.
For life and death are one,
even as the river and the sea are one.

Kahlil Gibran

Without birth and death, without the perpetual transmutation of all the forms of life, the world would be static, without rhythm, undancing, mummified. Every leaf must fall. If there is a deathless leaf it must be a plastic one. Do you want to live forever in an imitation plastic form of yourself? For what purpose? Death is necessary for the dynamic life to play in all its glory.

Swami Chinmayananda

Through new opportunities afforded by death and changing conditions, the soul is seeking its innate changelessness. And so never feels satisfied until it acquires and becomes reestablished in its natural state of oneness with Spirit. Therefore death, or change of the condition in which the soul temporarily resides, is conducive to the soul's growth and development.

Paramahansa Yogananda
The Divine Romance

I

Understanding Death

by Swami Suddhananda

At the beginning of a lecture series at a *Kalyāṇa Māṇḍapam* (a place where people marry), a friend of mine came to me and asked: "Swamiji, who is getting married here?" I said, "Today we are going to get married to Death."

There is, in reality, no question of not getting married to death. Instead, death is a beautiful, innocent bride, always trying to hang on to Me, the immortal, but I, in my ignorance, try to run away from death. There is not one individual who will ever run after death. It seems that death always runs after us. Every one of us tries to run away from it. Death is such a beautiful thing, but the most misunderstood phenomenon. If life is not understood, death is also completely misunderstood.

I shall begin with one of my childhood experiences. When I was studying in primary school, which was a few kilometers away from my home, I used to pass by an oil mill every day. On my way back, I used to sit on the wooden bar of the oil press and go for a ride with my friends. One day when we were coming back, we saw a big crowd in front of the oil mill, and everyone was looking sad. As children we were wondering what had happened and someone told us that the lady of the house died. We did not understand what it meant. We were only unhappy that we could not have a ride that day, and so we went back home. That night there was a commotion in the village and everybody was talking about the lady who had died and had come back to

life after two hours. As they were preparing her body for cremation, she suddenly came to life and got up. Everyone was fright-
ened, as they thought they were seeing a ghost.

The lady said, "I was dead for some time. I was taken away
and presented to a luminous being. He said, 'You have brought
the wrong person. Her time is not yet over. You go and leave her
and come back.' So I was left near the temple. I came from there
almost in a moment, and now I am up."

This is a true incident and the lady does not have any reason
to make up this story. Even now she is alive, about seventy-five
or seventy-six years old. At that time, I was not interested in
death, nor in life beyond death. Later when I went back to the
village, I asked the lady whether it was a true experience. She
clearly recalled all the details and said, "I am no more afraid of
death because I do know that I survive even after death."

What we call "death" is the end of the physical body. With
the body we are supposed to be born, with the body we are growing, and with the death of the body we think we die. In Sanskrit
the word "death" is called *naśa* (destruction) which means
adarśana, no more seen, not available for perception. Doctors
and scientists are interested as to the "why" of death. It is perhaps interesting to know why death occurs, but it is better to
know what death is, because "why death" is a question that will
lead to infinite regress.

Fear of Death Behind All Fears

If death is understood, there will be a complete change in
life as there will no more be fear of death. It is only the fear of
death which is reflected in all our fears of things and beings.
Anytime we are afraid of anything or any being, it is not the
thing itself we are afraid of, but it is the fear of death. Suppose I
say that I am afraid of my employer. It only means that if he is
not happy with me, he will dismiss me from my job, and I will
not have any money. If I do not have money, I cannot purchase

food and this means I will die. I fear my employer only because of this.

When I am afraid of a tiger, it is not the tiger that I am afraid of. I am afraid because he may jump on me and kill me. But the very same tiger in a cage evokes no fear in me as he cannot kill me.

Death is something certain in life. When a child is born, one never knows whether he is going to be a Nobel prizewinner or a criminal, but one thing is certain: he is going to die. One does not need an astrologer to predict this. It is a definite fact. It is a real tragedy that we always neglect this definite aspect of life and we become lost in the indefinite!

A person taking a management course was asked the following question: "Suppose you work in a factory, where there is the possibility of an accident one day in a year, which day should you be careful?" In three hundred and sixty-five days, the possibility of an accident is 365:1; now which day should you be careful? Naturally, you should be careful every day, because that day can be any day. The possibility of death in our life is in proportion of any second or any moment to all the eighty or a hundred years of life. But then that second could be any second, even before I finish this sentence I can collapse.

Everything Must End

Death is a definite event and it can happen at any moment. We have not taken care of this definite moment and we are planning for tomorrow's breakfast, the day after tomorrow's lunch, or for five years from now. There is nothing wrong in planning ahead. But nowadays our priorities have changed. We have given importance and priority only to living, without considering that "one definite moment." Living is, of course, a privilege but we must understand it and live in a far better way. Life will be far more interesting if we understand death, as there will no longer be a haunting, nagging fear in our lives.

Anytime when we say "death" we should not think only of the death of the physical body, but also death of many different events that affect us even more. Let us take the example of my talk here. The talk began at 6:45 p.m. Maybe it is very interesting, but however interesting it may be, if it does not come to an end, it will be terrible.

This is a *Kalyāṇa Māṇḍapam* and weddings take place here. A wedding is auspicious and wonderful. But suppose the wedding function never ends, will it still be interesting? That it ends is wonderful. The trouble is that we want certain enjoyable things not to finish, and we want unhappy incidents to finish quickly. That is how we become disappointed and totally dejected. The very fact that a particular thing begins, means that it has the seed of death in it. The very fact that it has come, means it also has to go. If it was not there before, it will not be in the future also. Everything is in a continuous flux, continuously moving. When something goes, we do not even have to say goodbye, because even without our saying anything, it rushes off. Similarly, when something comes we do not have to welcome it because it comes anyway, in spite of us, not because of us.

Thus, once the individual incidents are taken care of in our life, whether it is poverty or prosperity, life or death, disease or health, anything for that matter, if we accept it as it is, then the next thing is to try to understand what death is. When we do know it, our whole life-style will change.

Saint Tukaram's Secret

One day a devotee came to Saint Tukaram and asked him: "Maharaj, you are so open and free in life; you have no secrets. You never become angry with anyone, you are so cool, collected, and so together. How has that happened to you? Please tell me the secret of your life?"

Instead of answering his question, Tukaram said, "Look, I know a secret about you."

The man did not know what to say. He asked, "Maharaj, what is that?"

Tukaram said, "You are going to die in seven days."

As Tukaram was a great saint, the man could not disbelieve his words. He went back home and did all that had to be done in those seven days. He became wonderful with his wife and children because he had only seven days more to live, and he tried to be the very best that he could be. On the seventh day someone told Tukaram that the man was now going to die.

Tukaram went to see the man and asked, "Tell me what happened?"

The man said, "Maharaj, I am going to die now. Please bless me, pray for me."

Tukaram said, "All right, but how have you lived for the past seven days? Were you angry with your wife, children, or with your friends?"

The man replied, "Maharaj, how could I get angry with anyone if I were to die after seven days?"

Tukaram said, "Now you know my secret of keeping my mind cool, calm, and collected all the time. I remember that particular relationships can end at any moment!"

This was the secret of Tukaram's calm and peaceful mind. He knew that the next moment could be the last moment. He lived with an understanding and not with fear.

Death is not a frightening incident. In Sanskrit there is a very beautiful statement. It is said that when you meet a person, think as though you are meeting him for the first time. And when you are eating or enjoying something, think that you are enjoying it for the last time in your life. Do you see what this means?

We do not need teachers, philosophers, or missionaries to tell us that life is misery. We know that already. If teachers or scriptures have to say anything at all, they must tell us that life is so wonderful, it is not meaningless nonsense. If we find it meaningless, it is our own fault. We label something as good and something else as bad and then we suffer. In this creation everything has its own place.

The Nature of the Body

In Sanskrit the physical body is called *śarīra* or *deha*, that which is burned is *deha*. In Hindu tradition the body is burnt, in most of the other traditions the body is buried. When the scriptures say that this body is burnt, it does not mean that it is burnt by fire. The body is burnt by three *tapas* (problems in life).

That is why in our peace invocation we repeat *Om śāntih* three times. One *śāntih* takes care of suffering concerning the physical self. These are the problems that come out of the body, like disease, pain, pleasure, and so on. The second *śāntih* takes care of problems caused by the physical environment. Problems created by the people around us, by the types of government, or caused by beings like snakes, crocodiles, and so on. The third *śāntih* is for problems caused by the unknown, for example, while a person is walking he is hit by a thunderbolt, or from floods or droughts.

The physical body is continuously burnt or affected by these three *tapas*. That is why it is called *deha*. The other word is *sthūla śarīra*; *sthūla* means gross, and that which is continuously decaying and dying away is *śarīra*. Once we understand the nature of the body, we shall love this wonderful instrument. It is so fantastic. When we do not know the nature of something, it remains a mystery. If we understand how it works, we are no more affected by it. No one complains about the fire that burns. If it does not burn, there is something wrong with the fire, is it not? No one complains that sugar is sweet. If sugar is not sweet, what else will it be? So if the nature of a thing is known we have absolutely no reason to complain about it.

Look at the physical body and its nature. This body with which we are born has six modifications. It is in the potential state inside the father and mother, and is then born. It grows and undergoes changes as it goes through adolescence and so on. Then it starts decaying and dies away. These are the six modifications that the physical body goes through. The modifications do not begin after birth only. They start in the womb itself. On the day of conception the physical body starts growing, and continuous physical changes take place. Decay began from the very moment of conception as various cells died, and when the child leaves the womb to come into the world, there is death of another condition.

There are two schools of thought in astrology. One school says that the moment of the child's birth is the moment the child is born. Another school says the moment of the child's birth is the moment when the child is conceived. In the womb itself, the child has already started to grow, and death also takes place in the womb itself. If the child has developed friendship with the microbes in the world of the womb, naturally they will miss this huge microbe! They will suffer when the child comes out of the womb. This is the nature of the body. If the body does not grow, or does not change, something is wrong with it. If the body dies, there is nothing wrong. Is it not true that we begin to worry when a child turns seven or eight years old and has not yet grown enough? We start giving him all sorts of vitamins whether he assimilates them or not. We continue to feed him because he is not growing, but when he is dying, we are worried.

We have so many expectations! We want to reach up to our twentieth year, and after that no changes must take place. A particular stage of growth should come, and after that we must stop. No, even as we are enjoying the growth of the body when it is young, we must enjoy the decay of the body. And also welcome the time when it is ready to go. We are afraid, because we think that with the death of the physical body we also die. Once we know that even after death—death of the physical body—we survive, life will be a fantastic journey, so beautiful.

II

Reflections on Life and Death

by Swami Chinmayananda

There are some schools of thinkers who have established that death is the end of everything and there is nothing beyond it. There are others who accept, argue, and heartily proclaim that there is existence even beyond the grave. Most of us also show a keen interest in wanting to know what lies beyond. But only few of us apply ourselves to the practice of how to make our lives more fulfilling in the present moment. Yet understanding our present life is much more important than trying to discover what is after death. How to experience undisturbed peace and happiness in ourselves, and how to bring this newfound peace and harmony back to the world is of vital importance to us all. Nevertheless, in this modern era, where people consider themselves to be highly intellectual, there is great curiosity and preoccupation to know what lies beyond the death experience. This shows that what we cannot see or experience has significantly greater attraction for us. Before entering into the subject, we should first analyze the following questions: What is life? What is death? And who dies?

* * *

Q: What is life?

A: From the point of view of the materialist, life is an illogical and meaningless procession from birth to death. One who is constantly engaged in the pursuit of earning, procuring, and hoarding material wealth cannot have the required subtlety of mind to inquire into the possibilities of the hereafter. As long as the mind and intellect are drowned in the base values of life, which are built upon thoughtless conclusions and instinctive identification with one's body, one shall not easily entertain the urge to go beyond the shackles of mortal limitations. The materialistic person seems convinced that there is nothing after death, and firmly believes that death is the end, as no one has ever come back to talk about it.

But for spiritual students, life is a continuous process with a great purpose, a glorious pattern, and full of meaning. They understand that the life which they are living today is an effect, and since every effect must have a cause, their lives must have their independent causes, even though they may not be visible today. Spiritual life is a continuous attempt to live a divine life. Thus, the spiritual student tries to live up to certain higher values such as tolerance, love, kindness, and mercy.

* * *

Q: What is death?

A: Viewed from a scientific perspective, a person is considered to be alive when he is able to respond to certain stimuli that he receives through the sense organs. When an organism or individual stops responding to the stimuli, we say he/she is dead. Now let us analyze this, please. Who exactly is dead? We see that the body is still there; no part of it has gone away. The same body is lying there which was there before death. Yet, when we say Mr. X has died, what we really mean is that the mind and intellect which were receiving and responding to the outer stimuli have left the body. [The mind and intellect are expressions of thoughts in two different functions: feeling (mind) and thinking (intellect).] Hence, we conclude that Mr. X., the person who called himself "I" or "me," is other than the body. Though the physical body is still there, the mind and intellect have left it.

This physical body is composed of the five great elements: space, air, fire, water, and earth. It is the nature of the body to merge back with the same five elements when it is dead, meaning, when the mind and intellect have left it. Therefore, I must conclude that I am the possessor or the indweller of the body. The body is just like a tenement for which I pay rent in the form of food, three to four times a day. If I forget to pay the rent you can imagine what a tragedy I will have to meet with!

Similarly, this "dwelling" is but an instrument through which I express myself in this world, just like my car. If my car is destroyed, why should I think that I am destroyed? I am not the car. I am only the owner of the car. In the same way, if the body is destroyed, I am not destroyed. I am other than the body. My senses are only those instruments through which I receive stimuli from the outer world. Therefore, it is the mind and intellect which is the real individuality of a person. When we say we must develop the personality, we denote that the mind and intellect are to be developed. A truly cultured or civilized person is one who has a sharp and integrated mind and intellect. Due to our unintelligent ways of thinking, however, we do not look beyond the body.

* * *

Q: What is the difference between life and death? Matter activated by Consciousness is a living body. If Consciousness is not activated in a dead body, what happens to that Consciousness? Is it all-pervading? But if Consciousness is not present in a dead body, how can we say it is all-pervading?

A: Consciousness reflected in the mind and intellect (subtle body) is the consciousness of things. When the mind and intellect leave the gross body, it is the condition of death of the gross body. Since the subtle body alone can reflect infinite Consciousness, there is no apparent feeling, thinking, or perception for a dead physical body.

When, with a mirror, we reflect a pool of light A at a point on the wall and then tip the mirror, the specific pool of light A moves to B. We can now say the special individuality at A has gone (death) and a special individuality has come (born) at point B. But remember, the general sunlight that is on the wall has never "come" or "gone." When the special light created by the mirror at point A has moved away, the general light on the wall is still there, pure existence (*sat*) is in the dead body, but *cit* (knowledge) and *ānanda* (bliss) are not manifest in the dead body, as the subtle and causal bodies have left it.

* * *

The Question of Identification

Q: The sages proclaim that death is an easy and simple process, that it does not demand any effort on the part of the dying. They have told us that it is like going from one place to another. However, if this is so, why do we feel so sorry for an impending death, which is but going from one body to another?

A: This sorrow is due to our attachments for the objects of the world which we do not want to leave behind. Suppose I am sitting in the dining room and I tie myself to the table, chairs, and cupboards with a rope. If I then leave the dining room for the bedroom, I naturally invite discomfort, pain, and sorrow for myself.

One can frequently observe scenes of attachment at railway stations just before the time of the train's departure. A few persons will have tears rolling down their cheeks, some will have melancholy faces, and you may even see some of them running along with the train shouting, "Please write every day." This is all because of attachment.

Possessiveness or attachment is due to identification. In the waking state you identify yourself with the gross body. Therefore, you are conscious of it, and you think that happiness and sorrow of the body are your happiness and sorrow.

When you withdraw your identification from the gross body and identify with the subtle body, you are in the dream state. You do not experience any happiness or sorrow of the gross body, but you are happy or unhappy in the dream-world of experience, which was created by your mind and intellect.

When you have withdrawn your identification from the gross as well as from the subtle body and have identified with your causal body, you are in the deep-sleep state and not experiencing any happiness or sorrow of the gross or subtle bodies. There you experience undisturbed peace and bliss, but you are not conscious of your experience of peace and happiness. When you reach the fourth state of consciousness, called *turīya*, you have conscious experience of happiness which is your own nature.

As we have already discussed, when the subtle body takes the pilgrimage from a given physical body to another, we say that the person has died. Yet, each will continue to go on to such bodies as controlled by their desires, demands, or cravings. We remain in a certain place until our particular demands are met, and afterwards we leave that place and go to another where our next predominant desires are to be fulfilled.

You could say that the mind and intellect relationship with the body is something like that of a bird with its nest. The nest is safe as long as the bird continues to visit the nest to feed its young. But as soon as its purpose to visit is over, it flies away, never thinking about the nest. And without the bird, the nest perishes. There is no sense of possession or ownership in this.

Similarly, until the subtle body exhausts its desires, loves and hatreds, and likes and dislikes, the physical body is safe. When the purpose of the subtle body is exhausted, it leaves its physical frame. Without the subtle body, the physical body must perish. But actually we have not perished, for we are something other than the body.

* * *

Q: Why do we fear death?

A: Whatever be the span of life allotted, there is death lurking at the end of it all. Death is equally painful whether it be today or a thousand years from now. Everything that one has gathered, for which one has worked many hours each day, three hundred and sixty-five days of the year—the house, wife, children, name, and fame—we must leave one day. Because we lack correct knowledge of our real nature, we unintelligently create wrong relationships with the objects of the world. These relationships are called attachments.

But suppose there had been no death and only birth. What a tragedy! There would have been no more space available on the earth. An increase of only a few million people creates a headache for the government. Whether we like it or not, it is the benevolent law of nature that brings death. When we agree that death must come, why should we fear it?

We fear death because of our identification with the gross body and of gathering the qualities of the body on our Self. Our identification with the body is so strong that we apprehend destruction of ourselves whenever we think of the death of the body. Now the question is: Can the mind and intellect remain without the body?

Let us take the example of the relationship of the bullet and the gun. A bullet or a gun alone cannot frighten or kill us because by themselves they do not have any power. But when the bullet is in the gun, it certainly can frighten us. And when fired from the gun it can bring death. A bullet can only travel in the direction in which the gun is pointed. As long as the bullet is in the gun, the gun has control as to which direction the bullet will travel. Once the bullet is shot or has left the gun, the gun has no control over it.

Similarly, while our mind is in the body we have control over the mind. But once the mind and intellect have left the body, the body has no control over it. The mind will be shot in the direction decided by the sum total of our thoughts and activities of our entire lifetime.

* * *

Q: Why should we not indulge in the objects of the world during our lifetime, and contemplate upon the Lord only at the time of death?

A: This proves impossible, for how can we think of God in our final hours after focusing a lifetime of thoughts on the external world? It is therefore suggested that we should begin to contemplate upon God right here and now, for it is not certain when death will come. It is necessary for us to think of the Lord at the time of death because these thoughts provide us with a certain atmosphere and a proper vehicle to accomplish our voyage to perfection.

Therefore, to the intelligent person, death is not painful, but a new experience. If a candle is burned, nothing is lost. There is only a change in name and form. Similarly, nothing is lost in death to the person of wisdom. For him it is but a change of body, place, and time.

* * *

Q: Is there an interval between the departure from one body and entry into another?

A: This can be explained by the following example. When an officer is transferred from one city to another, say from Bombay to Delhi, he must first give up his charge and leave Bombay and then reach Delhi in order to take up his new appointment. He has handed over his duties at Bombay and is on his way to Delhi. If he is asked on the way if he is the officer, he will certainly confirm that, but when he is asked if he is an officer of Bombay or Delhi, he cannot answer, for, at that moment, he is neither in Bombay nor in Delhi. Yet he is still the officer inasmuch as he is getting paid for the interval period also. Therefore, the interval can be called the joining time.

Similarly, when the subtle body leaves a given physical body in order to assume a new one, there must be an interval between the two events. The duration of this interval depends upon the relationship that you have with the body that you are shedding and the urgency you feel for the next embodiment.

* * *

Q: Can we contact the dead?

A: In our scriptures it is said that we can contact the dead, but the rishis strongly advise against it. They say that by calling our loved ones back here, we are perhaps asking them to come down into a lower world. If, at that time, our loved ones are at higher realms of experience, we stop their pilgrimage by calling them down, and instead of sending their blessings they will curse us.

In this world also, no one wants to come down from a higher to a lower state. If one is forced to come down from a higher state he will be cursing those responsible for his fall. Similarly, why should the spirits respond to our call when they are in a higher realm? They do so because they are overpowered by their love and attachment for us. Some spirits, however, refuse to come down because they are not overpowered; thus they continue their pilgrimage to a higher plane.

We can observe similar incidents right here on earth as certain parents sacrifice their own principles in order to make their children happier. Say a young man wants to marry a particular girl, but his parents do not like the match. If, after much persuasion, the son still wants to marry the girl, the parents, though not happy, will sacrifice their happiness in preference to that of their son. This is because of their attachment to him.

Therefore, by calling the spirit of a dead person, we are not going to do any good for our dear ones. If we are not able to do something good for them, at least we should not harm them. It is now left up to each individual to think these ideas over and act intelligently.

III

The Grandest Truth

by Swami Tyagananda

Which truth is the grandest of all the truths in life? Every one of us may have a different answer to this question. Swami Vivekananda also answered this question once. He had put the question to a group of college boys who had gone to meet him. The boys were intelligent enough to keep their mouths shut, knowing that it was a rhetorical question and Swamiji's answer would soon follow, which it did. According to Swami Vivekananda, the grandest of all truths is, "We shall all die!"[1]

That does not sound like a very impressive answer, does it? Every one of us is going to die one day. Well, we all know that. We do not need a Vivekananda to tell us about it. The inevitability of our death is a truth all right, but the grandest of all truths? Ridiculous! It is rather the most unpleasant of all truths. It is a truth we would rather not think about. Instead of thinking about life and living it to the full, why should we fritter away our time and energy brooding over the gloomy, dark thought of death? Death is going to come anyway, whether we think about it or not. Why should we idolize this hideous truth and call it, of all things, the grandest of all truths? Swamiji's answer, therefore, seems at first sight to be either plainly absurd or meant as a joke.

In reality it is neither. When a Vivekananda speaks, thoughtful men and women do not dismiss his statements so easily. To hear the words of a prophet we need something more than merely a pair of good ears; to read a prophet's words in print we need something more than merely a pair of good eyes. That something more is humility, reverence, and a sensitive, truth-seeking heart. When the words of a prophet reverberate in the heart of such a person, their inner meaning is revealed.

Ceaseless Contemplation on Death

Let us now try to open our hearts to Swamiji's luminous words:

> Look here—we shall all die! Bear this in mind always, and then the spirit within will wake up. Only then will meanness vanish from you, practicality in work will come, you will get new vigor in body and mind. And those who come in contact with you will also feel that they have really got something uplifting from you.[2]

All this sounds most interesting. Swamiji puts as the prime condition that the grandest of all truths—the truth of our eventual death—must be kept in mind *always*. A small part of the mind must always remain soaked in the thought of death. What shall we gain from this ceaseless contemplation on death? Awakening of the spirit, disappearance of all meanness, practicality in work, new vigor in body and mind, and power to uplift others. But all these will come to us only if we face the thought of death courageously. This is important. A coward may brood over the thought of death always. But unlike the seeker of Truth, the coward does not choose to do it, he is forced to do it. His inner weakness and fear compel him to terrorize himself with the thought of death. Swamiji could tolerate and forgive everything but cowardice. When a disciple timidly suggested that serving others in this evanescent world was of no use because death is always stalking behind everyone of us, Swamiji flared up:

> Fie upon you! If you die, you will die but once. Why will you die every minute of your life by constantly harping on death like a coward?[3]

It is clear that Swamiji wanted contemplation on death to be a healthy exercise of the brave and the earnest, not a death-phobia of the wimp. It is true, however, that even in the case of the brave and the earnest; the immediate effect of meditation on death would certainly be despondency and dropping of the spirit. The benefits would surface only later. Swamiji agrees:

> Quite so. At first, the heart will break down, and despondency and gloomy thoughts will occupy your mind, but persist; let days pass like that—and then? Then you will see that new strength has come into the heart, that the constant thought of death is giving you a new life, and is making you more and more thoughtful by bringing every moment before your mind's eye the truth of the saying, "Vanity of vanities, all is vanity." Wait! Let days, months, and years pass, and you will feel that the spirit within is waking up with the strength of a lion. That the little power within has transformed itself into a mighty power! Think of death always and realize the truth of every word I say. What more shall I say, in words![4]

As always, Swamiji was only echoing the instruction of his guru, Sri Ramakrishna, who taught: "The world is impermanent. One should constantly remember death."[5] On another occasion Sri Ramakrishna said: "Do your duty in the world but remember that the 'pestle of death' will sometime smash your hand. Be alert about it."[6]

Teachings from Other Traditions

The importance of keeping the thought of death always before our mind's eye has been emphasized in many other religious traditions as well. Ansari (d.1088), a Persian Sufi Master and poet, said, "O man, remember death at all times." In Ecclesiastics (VII:40) we find this instruction: "In all thy works remember thy last end, and thou shalt never sin." Daidoji Yusan, (17th century), a samurai and author, wrote: "The idea most vital and essential to the samurai is that of death, which he ought to have before his mind day and night, night and day, from the dawn of the first day of the year till the last minute of the last day of it."

Takeda Shingen (1521-1573), a great Japanese general and student of Zen, remarked: "Zen has no secrets other than seriously thinking about birth and death." *The Imitation of Christ* expresses the idea this way: "Thou oughtest so to order thyself in all thy thoughts and actions, as if today thou wert to die."

It is important to remember that. Not only must there be the effort to keep in mind the thought of our death, but we must persist with this practice even through the dark, depressing days of despondency. Whenever perseverance, grit, and a strong will to succeed are present, light has to come sooner or later. That is what happens in the case of meditation on death also. If Nachiketa could remain doggedly resolute in his quest to know the secret of death, brushing aside all of Yama's alternate, tempting offers, it was because Nachiketa had for long contemplated on the fact of his own death. At the end of Yama's teaching, Nachiketa was an altogether transformed person. The form of a child remained, but his consciousness had smashed all barriers and become one with the universal Consciousness.

The thought of death was the turning point in Siddhartha's life too. On his maiden chariot-drive outside the palace, the young prince encountered disease, old age, and death. He might as well have driven on, dismissing these things as the inevitable facts of life that one has to somehow live with. That is what most of us do. If Siddhartha had also done that, he would not have become the great Buddha and he would not be remembered twenty-five centuries after he passed on. But the thought of human suffering, culminating in that climactic, mysterious event called death, never left Siddhartha's mind after what he saw outside the palace. When he solved the mystery years later under the bodhi tree, Siddhartha was a transformed figure. Gone was the prince of Kapilavastu and in his place stood the enlightened One, the prince of renunciation and compassion.

The passing away of Shivaguru, Adi Shankara's father, caused a profound change in the mind of young Shankara. Encountering the reality of death so early in life, the young boy began to view the world in an entirely new light. Life was never the same for him again. He never looked back until he had solved the mystery of death. Indeed, a Sanskrit movie on Shankara's life showed him always flanked by two companions, Knowledge and Death: Shankara had acquired the first, and conquered the second. Visible only to Shankara, these companions followed him everywhere. Toward the end of the movie, we see Death bidding farewell to Shankara. The great monk intuitively realized that the time had come for him to lay down the body and enter the infinite, indescribable realm of immortality.

A similar thing happened in the life of a boy named Ramakrishna, who lived at Kamarpukur, an out-of-the-way village in Bengal. He was only seven when his father Khudiram died. The whole family was plunged into sorrow. But the death of Khudiram affected Ramakrishna more fundamentally than it did others. To all appearances, there was little change in the merry, lively child, but inwardly a tremendous transformation had taken place. Not many knew that the young boy had begun to quietly slip away and wander alone in the Bhutir Khal cremation ground, and in other solitary spots in the village. This inner change, sparked by the event of his father's death, reached its logical culmination at Dakshineswar when Ramakrishna experienced the Truth that transcends death. Thousands in all parts of the world are today studying the life of Sri Ramakrishna and striving to put into practice his inspiring, powerful teachings, in order to conquer both life and death.

These are just a few examples to show how the persistent thought of death, instead of demoralizing and weakening a person, can cause a qualitative improvement in life. It cannot only uplift and strengthen the person but also waft him or her into the arms of the Immortal Being where death has no access.

The usual question arises: All the examples given are of

extraordinary people, all geniuses. How can this apply to us ordinary people? Vivekananda answers:

> The science of yoga tells us that we are all geniuses if we try hard to be. Some will come into this life better fitted and will do it quicker perhaps. But we can all do the same, the same power is in everyone.[7]

There is no such species called "ordinary people." Every one of us is extraordinary. No exception there. Each soul is not only potentially divine but also equally divine. The degree of manifestation of divinity may vary, but the quality of divinity does not. The same power, said Swamiji, is in everyone. It is up to us to decide with what intensity and toward which goal that power is to be directed. If it is directed toward the grandest of all truths, toward the thought of our death—a wonderful thing happens. Certain subtle changes take place within and our personality undergoes a radical process of transformation. At the end of it, the old person is dead and a new person takes his place.

The Old and the New Person

How is this new person different from the old one? Given below are a few major differences. In the following paragraphs "old person" is abbreviated to OP, and "new person" to NP, and for the sake of convenience both are called "he." Everything said about him is equally applicable to her too.

OP is strongly attached to the world—to his kith and kin, to his possessions, to his career and social status, to his likes, hobbies, and ideas. The strong intensity of his attachments results from the conviction (not always acknowledged) that the world is all that matters. He has neither the time nor the inclination to think of anything beyond. "Who knows what is beyond, and who is bothered anyway?" he says with a devil-may-care attitude. Or perhaps: "Let me make the most of what is right before my eyes. Let me now eat, drink, and be merry. There will be ample time to think about death when I grow old." Or putting on the cloak of a pragmatist, he says: "Wisdom lies in making hay while the sun shines. Here is life and let me enjoy it while it lasts. As to death, there is probably nothing beyond, just zilch." OP can even be a pseudo-devotee and may consciously or unconsciously give his attachments a religious color!

NP is different. He may have a semblance of attachment to the world, but it is not strong. His meditation on death has revealed to him that nothing lasts. Everything perishes sooner or later. Even his own body will one day either provide food to the worms underground or become a pile of ashes and merge into the soil. No sensible person gets attached to shadows. NP sees a shadowy world, so he remains free and unattached.

Reactions to Desire, Anger, and Fear

Attachment breeds desire. OP's attachments fill him with unending desires, big and small, gross and subtle, noble and ignoble. A mind full of desires is like a sheet of water full of ripples, eddies, and whirlpools. So OP is always restless and anxious. Where is peace for him? No sooner is one desire fulfilled than another pops up. It is an endless chain and OP is bound hand and foot.

NP, on the other hand, has been freed from his worldly desires because his mind's constant dwelling on death has convinced him that pursuit of desires is really the pursuit of death. It is a way of hastening the process of death, for the needless struggle to satisfy one's desires destroys the body and weakens the mind. So NP says no to all desires except one—the desire to know the mystery of death, and to explore the realm that transcends death, or in popular terms, the desire to know God. This is a higher desire—a super desire, if you like—which subsumes and overcomes all other desires. This is a special kind of desire because, unlike other desires, this one takes him along the road to freedom, not to bondage.

Anger and fear arise invariably in every desire-filled mind. When obstacles come to obstruct the satisfaction of OP's desires, he gets angry. This anger is manifested externally if OP is not strong enough to overcome the obstacle. If the obstacle is too formidable, OP seethes with anger within. Strong or weak, OP cannot avoid being filled with anxiety about the unknown hurdles that lie ahead. He lives with fear that somehow the object of his desire and attachment may never be his or it may desert him or be snatched away. It is really a wretched existence. That is OP's lot.

NP is free from both anger and fear. Having the truth of his own death firmly impressed on his mind, he finds it so pointless and foolish to be angry with anybody for any reason. We do not generally get to see a person on his deathbed blowing his top. That is the time to forgive and forget. And that is what NP does, although he is not on his deathbed. The mistakes that the dying man seeks to rectify during the final moments are rectified by NP even when he is in the best of health. Not only does he not get angry, he does not also fear anything. Having encountered the truth of death day after day, month after month, NP is free from fear. What everyone is afraid of most is death, and the thought of death has become NP's sought-after companion. Therefore, where is the question of fear?

Delusion

A life without a worthy ideal is a life of delusion. The only ideal that OP has in mind is to satisfy the desire that is uppermost in his mind at any given time. This ideal is not only worthless but also unattainable. It defies all logic. One would think that satisfying a desire would get rid of that desire. Oh no, it does not, it only strengthens the desire by producing another desire to repeat the experience. So OP lives an unfulfilled life.

NP's life has attained a measure of stability, because his ideal is to know the truth that transcends death. The uncertainties, incongruencies, and the hollow values of material life do not throw NP off his balance. The persistent thought of death invariably produces the thought of what transcends death. It is this constant plumbing of the depths of his mind with thoughts of the transcendent that lifts a person from the morass of delusion and gradually transforms him into an NP.

Thus, we see that while OP is bogged down by attachment, desire, anger, fear, and delusion, NP is absolutely free from them. This freedom leads to, as Vivekananda said, awakening of the inner spirit, disappearance of meanness, practicality in work, new vigor in body and mind, and power to uplift others.

Breaking Away

These are great assets, no doubt, but they are not the goal. The goal is to know the mystery of death. So with these newly acquired characteristics, which transform OP to NP, the person continues to quest for that which lies beyond death. Not for nothing did Swamiji call *sannyas* (renunciation) "love of death."[8] This should not be considered as meant only for those who embrace the monastic life. Every genuine spiritual seeker is a monastic, although only a few among these may get the inner call to receive the insignia of monasticism. While the monastic renounces both externally and internally, the lay seeker practices renunciation only internally. That is all the difference there is between a monastic spiritual seeker and a lay spiritual seeker. Undue emphasis has been laid on the differences between monastic life and lay life. It is not important whether a person is a monastic or a non-monastic; what really matters is whether the person is a true seeker of God. And that is easy enough to verify, for every true seeker loves death. Swamiji explains:

> Worldly people love life. The *sannyāsin* is to love death. Are we to commit suicide then? Far from it, for suicides are not lovers of death, as it is often seen that when people fail at trying to commit suicide they never attempt it a second time.

What is the love of death then? We must die, that is certain; let us die then for a good cause.[9]

Swamiji then goes on to show how the little individuality of ours, which is centered around the body and mind, must be replaced with a universal individuality that can embrace everyone and everything. The constant thought of death gives us that tremendous impetus to break away from the hold our narrow self has over us. It widens our consciousness and this finds expression as selfless, total love toward the entire creation. The spirit of service thus naturally fills the heart of an awakened soul. The body-mind-centered individuality of OP begins to fade away and its place is gradually taken by the God-centered individuality of NP. When this process is complete, an amazing change takes place. The thought "I will die one day" throws aside the veil over itself and we come face to face with the truth that proclaims "I will never die." The grandest of all truths, which reminded me every moment of my death, now takes me by the hand and leads me through the doorway to the absolute truth of my immortal nature.

OP felt "I will die one day" because his "I" was mixed up with his body and mind. NP realizes that "I will die one day" really means, "I will be separated from my body one day." The death that terrifies us all so much is nothing but the separation of the body from me and my mind. So it is really the death of the body, not my death, because I and my mind continue to live. Moreover, I do not have to remain bodiless forever. Soon enough I get another body. In the words of the *Gītā* (2:22), it is just like changing the old dress for a new one. The body-dress changes in every life. Since all of us have had millions of past lives, we have changed our dresses millions of times. Does it not now appear quite silly to make a big deal about such a simple matter as changing the dress? When we think about it calmly, death loses its terror for us.

What worries NP is not the death of the body but the survival of the mind! He knows that the real problem-generator is not the body but the mind. As long as the mind lives, it is going to latch on to somebody or other. It cannot live on its own for long, because all its desires need a body for expression and satisfaction. So NP longs for the death of the mind itself. He is fed up with his mind-dress and the numberless body-dresses he has worn and discarded. NP just does not want a dress anymore. In the Bible, man's fall is symbolized by his desire to cover himself. Man was born pure and naked. The first stain of impurity produced in him the desire to cover himself. NP has long since changed the direction of his journey. He is now swimming upstream toward God, having purified himself of all worldly desires. So clothes—the body-dress and the mind-dress—become superfluous. He wants to wander freely now in God's garden, pure and naked, like Adam. NP's expanding consciousness is no more able to remain confined within the body-dress and the mind-dress.

NP, however, does not go out of his way to seek the falling of the body-dress—he knows that eventually it is going to fall anyway, once its karma texture withers away. What NP strives to throw away with all his might is the mind-dress. The power to fling it away—or, more accurately, to burn it away—comes through the grace of God, which is ceaselessly blowing like a breeze; we have only to unfurl the sails of the yacht of our life. Meditating on the grandest of all truths is the first step in the process of unfurling the sails to catch the breeze of divine grace.

The burning away of the mind-dress is another kind of death. It separates NP not only from his body but also from his mind. This happens only once. NP is then free forever. No more deaths for him, because there are no more births for him. He then has no body and no mind—and so no limitations and bondage of any kind. No more can NP be referred to as he or she. Gender belongs to the body, not to the Self. NP is now the unfettered Self, free, perfect, and immersed eternally in supreme bliss. It is easy to understand now why Swamiji called the certainty of death as the grandest of all truths—for it takes us swiftly, as no other truth can, to the absolute Truth of our immortal, divine, and blissful nature.

FOOTNOTES:

1 *Complete Works of Swami Vivekananda*, 5:329 (hereafter cited as CW).
2 *Ibid.*
3 CW, 7:176.
4 CW, 5:329-30.
5 *The Gospel of Sri Ramakrishna*, 589.
6 *Ibid*, 428.
7 CW, 4:219.
8 CW, 3:446.
9 CW, 3:446.

IV

The Sufi Teachings on Death

by Hazrat Inayat Khan

The body is nothing but a covering put over our soul, and when it is gone we are not dead; just as we do not think that we are dead when our coat is worn out, or if someone tears our shirt. The moment when a person dies is the only moment when he feels that he is dead. The impression of his dying condition, the hopelessness of the doctor, the sorrow and grief of the family cause this impression. After death, as he recovers from this, he gradually finds himself alive; for the life that kept him alive in his physical garb, of course, feels strange without that garb. Yet it is not dead; it is even more alive, for that great burden has been removed, which for a time had made him think that the physical garb was his life.

The soul by its power has created the elements from itself, and has attracted them from outside. It has collected them and it holds them, but through use they are gradually worn out and last only for a certain period. The soul holds the body composed of all these elements as long as it has interest in the body. And as long as the magnetism of the body holds it, and its activity keeps it engaged. As soon as its interest in the body is lessened, or the elements which form the body have lost their power, by feebleness or some irregularity in the system, the body loosens its hold. And the soul, whose innate inclination is to free itself, takes advantage of this opportunity given to it by its bodily inability. The result of this is death.

The elements begin to disperse even before death, but after the death of the body they return straight to their affinity, earth to earth, water to water, and so on. And they are very glad to return. Each thing is glad to be with its own type. If there is gas near the fire, the flame will go out to the gas, because there is the fire-element in the gas.

One might think that this is all, and that after death there will be nothing left for the ordinary person who has thought of himself as this body, so tall, broad, heavy, or old; that when the physical body is gone all is gone. But it is not so; when the body is gone, the mind remains, the finer part of man's self, composed of vibrations. The elements exist in the vibrations and also in the atoms, otherwise a person who is angry would not get red-hot.

In dreams, when the body is asleep, we see ourselves walking, speaking, acting, in certain surroundings with certain people. It is only by contrast with the waking condition that we call it a dream. This self still exists after the body is gone, the exact counterpart of what we are now. Not what we were when we were five years old, or ten years old, but of what we are now.

It is sometimes said that the soul is that which remains after the death of the physical body, and that it is then in heaven or in hell, but that is not so. The soul is something much greater. How can that be burned with fire which is itself light, *Nur*, the light of God? But owing to its delusion, it takes upon itself all the conditions that the mind has to go through after death. Therefore the experience after death of the soul that has not attained to liberation is very depressing. However, if the mind is not much attached to the earthly life and has gathered up the satisfaction of its deeds, it enjoys heaven, if this is not the case it experiences hell.

HAZRAT INAYAT KHAN

The Weight of Earthly Attachments

The mind that is more involved in earthly cares and attachments cannot let the soul be in the light. If you throw a balloon into the air it will go up and then it will come down again. It goes up because of the air that is in it; it comes down because of the earth substance in it. The tendency of the soul is to go to the highest spheres, to which it belongs; that is its nature. The earthly substance it has gathered around it weighs it down to earth. The kite goes up, but the string in a person's hand brings it back to earth. Earthly attachments are the string that draws the soul downwards. We see that the smoke goes upward and on its way it leaves in the chimney its earth substance. All the rest of its earth substance it leaves in the air, and until it has left all behind, it cannot go up to the ether. By this simile we see how the soul cannot rise from the lower regions until it has left behind all earthly longings and attachments.

People have a great fear of death, especially the simple, tender, and affectionate people, those who are very much attached to their parents, siblings, and friends, and to their positions and possessions. Yet those who are unfortunate in life also fear death. A person would rather be very ill than dead. He would rather be in the hospital than in the grave. When the thought comes to a person, "Some day I must leave all this and go down to the grave," great sadness comes upon him. With some people this fear lasts part of their lives; with some it lasts a whole lifetime. The proof of how great the fear of death is, is that death has been made out to be the worst punishment, although it is not nearly as bad as the pains, sorrows, and worries of life.

Death is the great examination to which some go prepared, some unprepared, some with confidence, and others with fear. However much anyone may pretend to be spiritual or virtuous in life, at the moment of death he is tested and all pretense falls away. It is said in the Koran, "Then, when the crushing calamity shall come, on that day one shall remember what one has striven after."

There was an old man who was always crying and lamenting, saying, "I am so unhappy, my life is so hard, everyday toil and labor! It would be better if I were dead." Every day he lamented in this way and called upon death to come and take him. One day Azrael, the angel of death, appeared and said to him, "You have called me so often. Now I have come to take you with me." The old man said, "Not yet! I am an old man, pray grant me only a few days more of life!" The angel of death said, "No. You have so often asked to die, and now you must come to Allah." The old man said, "Wait a little while. Let me stay here a little longer." But the angel of death said, "Not one moment more," and he carried him off.

Importance of Self-Development

What thought should the mind hold at the moment of death? The thought should be according to the evolution of the person, either of God, or the object of his devotion, or pleasant surroundings, or whatever he has idealized. If he is an earthly person then the thought of pleasant surroundings will make a heaven for him. If he is in a state of devotion, he will unite with the object of his devotion. If he thinks of the divine, the thought of God will be right for him. "Verily death is the bridge that unites friend to friend" one finds in the Sayings of Muhammad. Those of whom it is said that they are in the presence of God, are those who hold the vision of their divine beloved whom they have idealized all their life. They rejoice for a long, long time in the presence of their idealized one.

During our life on earth we are conscious of three conditions: that of the body, the mind, and the soul. After physical death we are conscious of only two. On the physical plane, if a thief comes, we are not so afraid. We try to find something to attack him with, but in a dream we are afraid, for we have nothing with which to attack him. Here on earth the will is much stronger; there the imagination is stronger, and the will not as strong. In the physical life we have changes from one experience to another. If we are afraid in the night, we can say in the morning "I had a nightmare," or, "in my dream I was sad, but it means nothing." But there we have no change.

It is here, therefore, that we should awaken to what is the aim of our life. There we cannot improve as much as we can here. That is why there have always been some, the chosen ones of God, who have said, "Awake, awake while there is time!"

There are some who can do what they wish in a dream. They can make anything happen, and the next day they see what they saw in the night, but such are exceptional cases. Because they have mastered their will here, they can make everything go according to their will even on the higher plane.

When a person is just as glad that another should eat a good dish as that he should eat it himself, or that another should wear beautiful clothes like he would himself, then he is raised above humanity. These are the saints and sages, and their hereafter is in their hands, because they are happy, both in the gain and in the loss. The minds of the prophets and murshids cannot be compared with other minds. Theirs is a master mind, as they have lived only for others, and after death they still live for others. They have thought only of what is eternal. Others have thought of things that pass away, and so in time their mind passes away.

The Ocean of Eternal Life

Sufism is learned chiefly in order that a person may know what will happen to him or her after death, in that being which is our real being, though usually it is hidden from us. The life that cannot die can bear one up after the physical death and one can remain always alive. We living beings exist on earth and on the sea, having both elements in our form, the earth and the water. The beings of the sea are formed of earth as well; we also have water in our constitution. Yet the sea is as strange to us as the earth is to the creatures of the sea. Neither would like their places exchanged, and if it so happens that they are out of their element, it leads them to their end. It is because the fish has not realized that it is also an earthly being and that the earth is its element too, that it cannot live on earth. In the same way, beings on land whose life depend on getting to the shore, fail when they believe that they will sink in the sea.

If we were dropped into the sea, it would be a terrible thing. We would be convinced that we would go to the bottom, and that we would be drowned. It is our fearful thoughts that make us go to the bottom. There is no other reason we should sink. The sea lifts up the whole ship in which a thousand people are traveling and in which tons of weight are loaded; why should it not lift up our little body?

Our inner being is like the sea, our external being is as the earth. So it is with the word called death. It is the sea part of ourselves, where we are taken from our earth part, and, not being accustomed to it, we find the journey unfamiliar and uncomfortable, and we call it death. To the seaman the sea is as easy to journey upon, whenever he chooses to, as the land. Concerning this subject, Christ said to Peter, "O thou of little faith, why does thou doubt?"

Both in Sanskrit and Prakrit, liberation is called *Tāran*, which means swimming. It is the power to swim which makes water the abode of the earthly fish. And for those who swim in the ocean of eternal life, in the presence as well as in the absence of the body, it becomes their everlasting abode. The swimmer plays with the sea. At first he swims a little way, then he swims far out. Then he masters it, and at last it is his home, his element, as the earth is. He who has mastered these two elements has gained all mastery. The divers in the port of Ceylon, and the Arabs in the Red Sea, dive down into the sea. First they plug up their ears, eyes, lips, and nose, then they dive down and bring up pearls. The mystic also dives into the sea of Consciousness by closing his senses from the external world and thus he enters into the abstract plane.

The work of the Sufi is to take away the fear of death. This path is trodden in order to know, while in life, what will be with us after death. It is said in the Koran: "Die before death." To take off this mortal garb, to teach the soul that it is not this mortal but that immortal Being, so that we may escape the great disappointment that death brings, this is what is accomplished in life by a Sufi.

V

The Story of Emery Bord

by Arthur Hope

Once upon a time there was a little boy named Emery Bord who could hardly wait. Like most little boys, he could hardly wait to get into kindergarten. "Gosh," he would say, "school will be fun." Of course, once he got into kindergarten, he could hardly wait until he was promoted to the first grade so he would not be just a little kindergartner anymore. Once in the first grade, he could hardly wait to be in the second grade so he could play in the middle yard. As soon as he was in the second grade, he could hardly wait. . . . .

Well, by the time he was in the fourth grade, young Emery, like many, many little boys, loathed school. He could hardly wait for the morning recess. Then he could hardly wait for the noon recess. Then he could hardly wait for the afternoon recess, but hardest of all was waiting for the final bell.

"It will be different when I get to high school. I will have a car and dates and things," he said, "boy, I can hardly wait."

But high school was not much better. What he looked forward to now was going off to college. He could hardly wait.

Naturally, his grades were only mediocre. So he could only go to a mediocre college. Like many, many students, he found his professors a bore and his studies dull. He could hardly wait for midterm to be over and then finals to be over. He could hardly wait for Thanksgiving recess, Christmas recess, and Easter recess. And hardest of all each year was waiting for June.

What he really looked forward to was getting out in the world, getting married, and getting a job. "Oh, to be finished with school forever," he said, "I can hardly wait."

So at last he got out in the world, got married to a girl named Imogene, and got a job. He got a job with the Monolith Corporation as a memoranda processor. And like many, many of his fellow workers, he loathed it. As soon as he was at his desk, he could hardly wait for his morning coffee break, then his lunch-hour, and then his afternoon coffee break. And the hardest thing of all was to wait for the clock, which he glanced at constantly, to tick to 5:15.

Naturally, he was a charter member of the *Thank Goodness It's Friday Club*. Every Monday morning he would arise with a groan, counting the days that lay between him and the coming weekend, for which he could hardly wait.

Not only did Emery Bord count the hours and the days, but the weeks and the months as well. "Only three months and two weeks till my vacation, he would say to Imogene, "I can hardly wait."

And as he grew older, he began counting the years as well. "Do you realize that in only twelve more years I can retire?" he would say to Imogene. "I will never have to work again."

"I bet you can hardly wait, dear," she would reply. So the hours, days, weeks, months, and years finally passed. Old Emery Bord retired. He found he had a lot of time on his hands. He could hardly wait for the Monday night football game or the one drink his doctor allowed him before dinner or. . . . . Well, one evening, he clutched his chest and collapsed in his chair.

"Don't worry, dear," said Imogene, fluttering around him anxiously. "The doctor will be here soon."

"I can," gasped old Emery Bord, breathing his last words, "hardly wait."

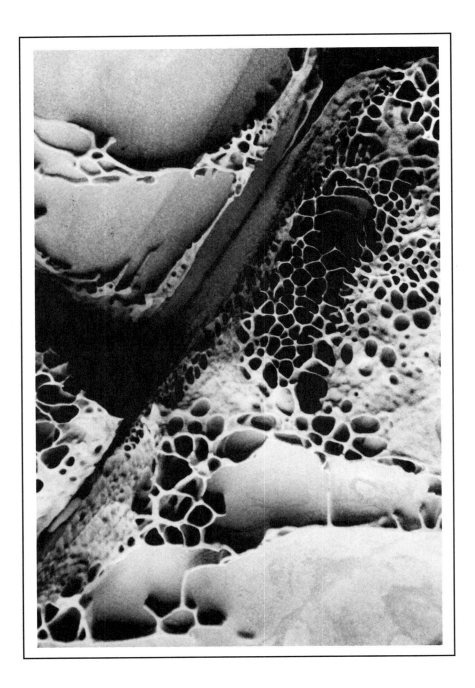

PART TWO

Overcoming Fear of Death

I died as a mineral and became a plant
I died as a plant and rose to an animal
I died as an animal and I became a man.
Why should I fear?
When was I less by dying?

Rumi

My belief in the power of the divine Spirit has grown, my fear of death has gone. I suppose I could say I am a changed person. I have lost interest in the church, but feel close to something powerful and divine, and I am also very aware of this influence on my thoughts and actions. I want to understand. I want to go back with knowledge. As I look back I find it interesting to note that for years I thought that the being bathed in light was Universal Intelligence. Not until after reading of other experiences did it occur to me to think of this person as any religious symbol.

Case 51
Ken R. Vincent
Visions of God from the
Near Death Experience

Knowledge is strength. When you know a thing you mastered it, but as long as you do not know it you are afraid of it. And fear of death proceeds from that ignorance, because you do not know what is meant by death and what will happen after death. The moment we know it, we become free from that fear. Therefore, one who knows that Master, that Ruler of the past and future, Ruler of the body and mind, who is dwelling in the center of the heart, small in size, has become free from death. And that Ruler of the body, mind, intellect, and senses is immortal.

Swami Abhedananda
Mystery of Death

VI

Cultivating Friendship With Death

by J. P. Vaswani

[The following article has been reprinted from Life After Death, *which contains a series of transcribed talks by the author.]*

Death is truly a friend and I would wish every one of you to cultivate friendship with death. Death is coming closer to us with the passing of each day. We live in an uncertain world, but one thing we all are certain of is the fact that one day we shall die. We are here on a return ticket. The probable dates of our return are stamped on the ticket, but we are unable to read them. We do not know when and where death will come and claim our body. Every day draws us closer to the day of death. Therefore, I would wish you to cultivate friendship with death. Once we have made friends with death, we shall not be afraid of it, but we shall continue to smile even while facing it.

In ancient India, this was the teaching that was passed on to every student. The student in ancient India was called a *jijñāsu*, a seeker after Truth. To the seeker after Truth, the rishi, the teacher, said: "My child, every day, for some time, meditate on death!" I would also wish this for every one of you. The day is coming when this body will die, the body of which we make so much, the body of which we are so proud, the body with which many of us are so identified that we think that it is all we are. The day is coming when this body will die. Where will we be then? We shall continue to exist. We have existed before our bodies were born. For all of us are more ancient than the hills, more ancient than the earth on which we have built our temporary habitation. If we meditate on death, we shall no longer be afraid of death. We shall then know that death is only an illusion; death is only an appearance. In reality there is no death. We cannot die.

Sadhu Vaswani, whom we in love and reverence call Beloved Dada, likened the death of the body to the sunset, he said to us: "Sunset is only an appearance, for what is sunset here is sunrise elsewhere. In reality, the sun never sets. Likewise, there is no death. Death is only an illusion, an appearance. For death here is birth elsewhere."

"What is death?" is the question which we put to Sadhu Vaswani once. He said, "Death is a bridge!" Yes, death is a bridge between the physical world and the astral world. When death comes, we leave the physical world and pass over the bridge to enter the astral world, which is a better, nobler, richer, more beautiful, more radiant world. . . .

On another occasion we again asked the same question: "What is death?" He said, "Death is a door!" Death is a door that leads from one room to another. It was Jesus who said: "In my Father's house are many mansions." One mansion is the physical plane, the earth plane. There are other mansions; there are other worlds, and death opens the door to those other worlds. John Masefield, the Poet Laureate of England, says in one of his poems, "Death opens unknown doors. It is most grand to die!"

Our dear ones who have passed away are not dead. They have but moved on through the door of death to another world. There they await our coming. We shall also follow them one day. When the time comes for us to leave this body, our dear ones will come and receive us at "the railway station," just like when we arrive at a new place. In the new journey on the other side we are not alone.

So it is that you might have found the faces of dying persons light up with radiant joy. They might have passed through physical pain and agony during the period of their illness prior to death. But when the last moments arrive, their faces are usually lit up with wondrous joy. Some of them even sit up and stretch out their arms. Some of them call out the names of loved ones who had previously died. Dr. Leslie Weatherhead, who studied this subject, tells us in his book, *After Death*: "I have never seen any one in any kind of distress at the moment of passing."

I read of a woman who had been unconscious for sometime. Suddenly, she sat up, held out her arms and said: "Oh my mother, my mother! Isn't she pretty?" The son of the dying woman was close by. He came and put his arms around his mother to lay her down, but she tried to reach out farther and said: "Let me go! My mother has come to receive me!" Saying those words, she lapsed into the sleep of death. At the time of death we are not alone. Our dear ones, who have gone before us, come and receive us.

My revered mother, who passed away about twelve months ago, said to me more than once: "I am not afraid of death, for half of my relatives are here, and half of them are there. When I make the transition, I will not be alone; I will be in the midst of dear ones." Before she dropped her physical body, she passed through a period of excruciating pain, but the last moments of her earth-life (I was present by her bedside) were peaceful. A strange, wondrous light shone in her eyes. . . .

It is enough if we take with ourselves this one thought: that we must not be afraid of death, for we do not die. It is the physical body that dies, and we have other bodies in which we continue to live after the death of the physical body. In the moment of our so-called death, we are not alone. In our new journey, we are taken care of at every step.

Let us also take with ourselves the thought that death is a door, death is a bridge, between the physical world and the astral world. . . . In the astral world are our dear ones. From there they look at us. They would love to reach us and tell us that life on earth is a preparation for the life that is to come.

Preparing for the Life Beyond

So let each day of our earth-life be a day of preparation. Prepare! Prepare! This is the one word that our dear ones on the other side wish to say to us. Prepare! Prepare! For they find us chasing things that, to them, are no better than shadow-shapes. They find us running after money, trying to accumulate wealth, yet not a single penny of which we will be allowed to carry with us into the great beyond. They find us running after pleasures and sense-enjoyments, after name and fame, and power. These are all shadows. So they ask us to open our eyes, to wake up from the slumber of the senses and the mind and prepare for the inevitable journey.

Here are three practical suggestions as to how we should prepare for the life that is to come. Life on earth is transitory, momentary. When we drop the physical body, we shall feel as though we have awakened out of a dream. Then this entire life, which now appears to be so long—in some cases interminable —appears to be but a moment in eternity. Let us make the most of this life and each day prepare for our life in eternity.

Suggestion number one is this: Establish a link of love and devotion with Krishna, Rama, Buddha, Jesus, Muhammad, Mahavira, or Moses, with a saint, a man of God, who to us, is God Himself. Everyday let us strengthen this link of love and devotion. Every day, let us pray to God, let us kiss God's holy feet, let us offer all our work to God. Let us, in moments of silence, converse with Him in love and with intimacy. Let this link grow, from more to more, until we feel that wherever we are, we are not far from God, we are overshadowed by His radiant presence. And in His presence there can be no death. For when the body dies, He will be beside us and lift us into His loving, everlasting arms, leading us on—ever onward, ever forward, ever Godward!

Practical suggestion number two: As we establish this link of love and devotion with God, we shall realize that in everything that happens there is a meaning to God's mercy. Many things happen in life: we are unable to understand why they happen. Suddenly our dear ones are snatched away from us, or a calamity befalls us, or a misfortune overtakes us. Instead of wasting our time and energy inquiring why bitter experiences come into our life, let us move forward to greet every incident and accident, every illness and calamity, with the words that Sadhu Vaswani gave us once, words that have become the mantra of my life: "I accept! I accept!"

Remember, friends, in the Divine Providence, nothing happens that does not happen for the good. And nothing comes a moment too soon or too late, but everything comes in its own true time. God's clock is never too slow. We do not see the Providence at the time. Not until afterwards may it be shown that our disappointments, hardships, trials, and the wrongs inflicted on us by others are part of God's good Providence toward us, full of blessing. Everything that happens to us comes to bless us and lead us onward in our way. Therefore, wherever God keeps me, let me remain. Wherever He sends me, let me go! Let me seek refuge at His lotus-feet, surrendering all my problems to Him, knowing that in God is a solution to all my problems. Let me greet every happening with the words: "I accept! I accept!"

Live Unselfishly

Practical suggestion number three: How should I express it? Be a blessing to others. In the measure in which you become unselfish, in that measure your heart expands. Those that lead selfish lives on earth, those that harm others in order to get little advantages, find themselves imprisoned in tiny, dark cells, when they move to the other side. Therefore, live unselfishly, be a blessing to others. God has blessed you with wealth and abundance, with position and power, so that you may be a blessing to others. Receiving without giving makes a person proud and selfish. Give out the best in you, in God's name, for the good of others. Give help to those who need it. Try to lighten the load of others.

I recall the words of Sadhu Vaswani. He said, "Did you meet him on the road? Did you leave him with the load?" Do not leave those whom you meet with the load that they carry on their shoulders. Lighten their loads, and remember, the loads are not merely physical. For the hearts of many are unhappy, burdened with worries and anxieties. Bring joy into the lives of those that are joyless. Give comfort to those in need of comfort. Be ready to serve, at any cost, those that require your service. Never forget for a moment that life and all its bounties are given to you as a trust, to be spent in the service of the poor and needy, in the service of brother birds and animals.

Friends, my time is almost over. I must bring my talk to a close. Establish a link of love and devotion with God or a God-man. Move forward to greet every experience in life with the words: "I accept!" And be a blessing to others. Starve that others may eat. Keep awake that others may sleep. And death cannot touch you. You will have entered into the life that is deathless, the life that is eternal.

In a hospital in France two persons were on their deathbeds. One of them was the world-famous author, Voltaire. His books are still studied in colleges and universities. There he lay on his deathbed. Around him were doctors and nurses doing their best for him. They found agony written on his face. He cried repeatedly, "What will happen to me now? I see nothing but darkness before me!" Voltaire had written many books, but he had not established a link of love and devotion with God. In the moment of death he felt lonely and lost.

In the same hospital, in another room, was a little girl. She was twelve years of age. She, too, was about to die, but she was happy, calm, and peaceful. Her face was wreathed in smiles. The doctors and nurses wondered at her serenity as they thought of the great man in the other room in the throes of fear. They said to her, "Little one! You know you are about to die, and you keep on smiling. Are you not afraid of death?"

This little girl, in her childlike innocent way said, "Why should I be afraid of death? My beloved Jesus is here, standing in front of me with outstretched arms. He says to me, 'My child, come unto me!'"

The little girl had established a link of love and devotion with Jesus. She was not afraid of death. As she passed away, on her lips was a song, which I have translated as follows, "The Beloved is near: I have no fear! In His arms I rest. Whither? He knows best!"

Where will He take me? He knows best. I only know that, wherever He takes me, He will keep me close to Himself—and that is all I need. For in Him is peace and joy, the peace that passeth understanding, the joy that knows no end.

Friends, I shall now finish my speech. May you be blessed and may your humble servant be blessed, that we may establish a link of love and devotion with God or a God-man, allowing us to greet every happening with the words, "I accept!" May we become a blessing to as many as we can, as we go along the difficult pathways of life, so that in the moment of death we can also sing the song that was on the lips of this little innocent girl.

VII

The Awakening of
Ramana Maharshi

by Arthur Osborne

When the Maharshi, Bhagavan Sri Ramana, realized the Self, he
was a lad of seventeen in a middle-class Brahmin family of
South India. He was still going to high school and had under-
gone no spiritual training and learned nothing of spiritual philosophy. Normally some study is needed, followed by long and
arduous training, often lasting a whole lifetime, and is more often still incomplete at the end of a lifetime. As the sages say, it
depends on the spiritual maturity of a person. It can be compared to a pilgrimage, and a day's journey on this pilgrimage to
a lifetime. How near a person comes to attaining the goal will
depend partly on the energy with which he presses forward and
also partly on the distance from it, at which he wakes up and
begins his day's journey. Only in the rarest cases is it possible,
as with the Maharshi, to take a single step and the goal is
reached.

To say that the Maharshi realized the Self does not mean that
he understood any new doctrine or theory, or achieved any
higher state or miraculous powers. But that the "I" who under-
stands or does not understand doctrine, who possesses or does
not possess powers became consciously identical with the
Ātman, the universal Self or Spirit. The Maharshi himself has
described in simple, picturesque language how this happened.

ARTHUR OSBORNE

The Great Change

It was about six weeks before I left Madura for good that the great change in my life took place. It was quite sudden. I was sitting alone in a room on the first floor of my uncle's house. I seldom had any sickness, and on that day there was nothing wrong with my health, but a sudden violent fear of death overtook me. There was nothing in my state of health to account for it, and I did not try to account for it, or to find out whether there was any reason for the fear. I just felt, "I am going to die" and began thinking what to do about it. It did not occur to me to consult a doctor or my elders or friends; I felt that I had to solve the problem myself, there and then.

The shock of the fear of death drove my mind inward and I said to myself mentally, without actually framing the words: "Now death has come; what does it mean? What is it that is dying? This body dies." And I at once dramatized the occurrence of death. I lay with my limbs stretched out stiff as though *rigor mortise* had set in and imitated a corpse to give greater reality to the inquiry. I held my breath and kept my lips tightly closed so that no sound could escape, so that neither the word "I" nor any other word could be uttered. "Well then," I said to myself, "this body is dead. It will be carried stiff to the burning ground and there burnt and reduced to ashes. But with the death of this body am I dead? Is the body 'I'? It is silent and inert but I feel the full force of my personality and even the voice of the 'I' within me, apart from it. So I am Spirit transcending the body. The body dies but the Spirit that transcends it cannot be touched by death. That means that I am the deathless Spirit." All this was not dull thought; it flashed through me vividly as living truth that I perceived directly, almost without thought-process. "I" was something very real, the only real thing about my present state, and all the conscious activity connected with my body was centered on that "I." From that moment onwards the "I" or Self focussed attention on Itself by a powerful fascination. Fear of death had vanished. Absorption in the Self continued unbroken from that time on. Other thoughts might come and go like the various notes of music, but the "I" continued like the fundamental *śruti* note that underlies and blends with all the other notes.[1] Whether the body was engaged in talking, reading, or anything else, I was still centered on "I." Before that crisis I had no clear perception of my Self and was not consciously attracted to It. I felt no perceptible or direct interest in It, much less any inclination to dwell permanently in It.

Such an experience of identity does not always, or even normally result in liberation. It comes to a seeker but the inherent tendencies of the ego cloud It over. Henceforward, he has the memory, the indubitable certainty, of the true State, but he does not live in It permanently. He has to strive to purify the mind and attain complete submission so that there are no tendencies to pull him back again to the illusion of limited separative being.

However, the Self-oblivious ego, even when once made aware of the Self, does not get liberation, which is Self-realization, because of the obstruction of accumulated mental tendencies. It frequently confuses the body with the Self, forgetting that it is in truth the Self. The miracle was that in the Maharshi's case, there was no clouding over, no relapse into ignorance. He remained henceforward in constant awareness of identity with the one Self.

FOOTNOTE:

[1] *The monotone persisting through a Hindu piece of music, like the thread on which beads are strung, represents the Self persisting through all the forms of being.*

VIII

The Consolation of the Bhagavad Gītā

by Swami Chinmayananda

An old woman once approached Lord Buddha with the dead body of her only son and pathetically implored him to give the child back his life. The Lord of Compassion was much moved by her sorrow. He consoled her by saying that if she would obtain a handful of mustard seeds from any house where no death had ever occurred, he would bring her child back to life. Without realizing the import of his great words the poor woman went from house to house begging for the mustard seeds in vain. She finally came to realize that there is no living thing that is not subject to death. She learned the truth that irrespective of power, position, and wealth, death deals impartial blows on one and all, that death is the leveler of all.

Death and birth are two phases of the same phenomenon called "change." Only from the death of the old can the new emerge. Old order changes, yielding place to the new. But in nature this process proceeds so smoothly and harmoniously that we, as casual observers, fail to notice the subtle motion of this mighty wheel of change. Morning matures to become noon, and noon steadily grows to be evening. Evening silently modifies itself to play as night, and the night has to end necessarily yielding its place to the dawn. Autumn precedes winter that moves on to meet spring and spring itself slowly merges into summer. Thus, the circle of seasons is formed, each following the other in perfect rhythm and order, with precision and harmony.

Youth emerges when childhood passes away, and youth in its turn hands us over to middle age. As time passes we grow into old age and finally reach the inevitable end called death. Buds mature into flowers, flowers fulfill themselves in fruits, and fruits must die and decay if the seeds are to sprout. This flow of change is noticed not only in the physical realm but also in the mental and intellectual realms. Immature thoughts and ideals end through education and other experiences in life. From thoughtless childhood we grow up into the reckless age of vigorous youth, and soon arrive at a more mature age when our thoughts are wiser and actions more purposeful.

If not for birth and death following each other with such irresistible regularity, all glamour would have been lost from life; nor would there be any beauty left in nature. Without change, life would end in absolute stagnancy. In spite of our appreciation of all these ideas, when death actually comes to extinguish the flame of life in a loved one, we suddenly realize that something is lost forever. In the ensuing sorrow and gloom we are not able to understand that death is also nothing but a continuation of that nonstop whirl of the irresistible wheel of change. In the general ignorance of the benevolent play of birth and death, we try to cling to one particular spoke of the wheel, usually with obstinate tenacity. Under this veil of illusion, we also come to suffer an unending measure of sorrow, for the wheel of change never stops.

The great archer and noble prince Arjuna, the hero of the *Bhagavad Gītā*, found himself perplexed and scared at the prospect of killing his near and dear ones on the battlefield of Kurukshetra. In that one sweep of overwhelming anxiety, all his former values dropped from him and he imagined himself to be the doer of his actions. Thus burdened, Arjuna found himself incapacitated to face the destruction of his elders, friends, and teachers. It is to this confused and anxious individual that the *Gītā* addresses itself as follows:

> *You have grieved for those that should not be grieved for;*
> *yet, you speak words of wisdom. The wise grieve neither for*
> *the living nor for the dead. Never was a time when I was not,*
> *nor you, nor these rulers of men. Nor, verily, shall we ever*
> *cease to be hereafter.* (II:11,12)

The Theory of Reincarnation

Krishna here declares in unequivocal terms that the embodied self is set on a great pilgrimage in life. This is where it comes to identify itself temporarily with a physical body to gain various experiences. He says that we do not suddenly come from nowhere, nor do we, at the moment of death, become mere nonexistent nothings. Correct philosophical thinking guides our intellect to the apprehension of a continuity from the past, through the present, to the future. The Spirit remaining the same, It identifies with different body-mind-intellect equipment, and thus comes to live in a particular environment ordered by Itself. This conclusion of the Hindu philosophers leads to the most satisfactory Theory of Reincarnation. All honest thinkers of the past and the present have accepted, expressly or tacitly, these logical conclusions.

Buddha constantly referred to his previous births. Virgil and Ovid regarded the doctrine as perfectly self-evident. Josephus observed that the belief in reincarnation was widely accepted among the Jews of his age. Solomon's *Book of Wisdom* says: "To be born in a sound body with sound limbs is a reward of the virtues of the past lives!"

Who does not remember the famous saying of the learned son of Islam: "I died out of stone and I became a plant; I died out of the plant and became an animal; I died out of the animal and became a man. Why then should I fear to die? When did I grow less by dying? I shall die out of man and shall become an angel!"

In later times, this most logical belief has been accepted as a doctrine by the German philosophers Goethe, Fichte, Schelling, and Lessing. Among the recent philosophers who have recognized this doctrine as incontrovertible are Hume, Spencer, and Max Mueller. Among the poets of the West, Browning, Rossetti, Tennyson, and Wordsworth come to mind, whose burnished intellects soared into the cloudless sky of imagination. Within their poetic flights they too intuitively felt the sanction for the continuity of life.

The Reincarnation Theory is not a mere dream of philosophers, and the day is not far off when, with the fast-developing science of psychology, the West will come to rewrite its scripture under the sheer weight of observed phenomena. To be logical we must accept the idea of the continuity of the embodied souls. An uncompromising intellectual quest for understanding life cannot satisfy itself if it is thwarted at every corner by "observed irregularities." We cannot, for long, ignore them all as mere chances.

The prodigy Mozart, for instance, is a spectacular example that cannot be explained in any other way. This genius wrote sonatas at the age of four, played in public at the age of five, and composed his first opera at the age of seven. Without the Reincarnation Theory, we must label this wondrous incident as an accident of nature and throw it into the heap of chance and bury it there. Examples are often quoted, but rarely recorded as evidence. The world today has yet to discover this great and self-evident Law of Life.

To the uninitiated student, however, this theory may seem to be too much. When Krishna declared that none of them, including Himself, Arjuna, and the great kings, even after their deaths on the battlefield "shall cease to exist in the future," Arjuna, a typical man of the world, could not grasp it as a self-evident fact. His questioning eyes made the Lord explain again the idea through an example in the following stanza:

Just as in this body the embodied (soul) passes into child-
hood, youth and old age, so also he passes into another
body; the firm man does not grieve at it. (II:13)

According to the law of memory, the experiencer and the memorizer need to be the same entities. Only then can memory-power function. I cannot remember any of your experiences, neither can you remember any of mine. Yet I can remember my experiences as readily and easily as you can remember your own.

This stanza is again asserting, in unequivocal terms, the truth behind the Reincarnation Theory. We do not bemoan the death of childhood when we come to experience youth. We know that even though youth is reached and childhood has ended, there is a continuity of existence of the same person. Thus, youthfulness may be considered as a birth, after child-hood has met with its death, and old age is born when youth dies. Yet, we are not the least disturbed by these changes. We feel happier due to the wealth of experiences we have gained, as the status of the individual rose from innocent childhood to mature old age. By using the subjective experience of everyone in the world as a standard of comparison, Krishna is here trying to point out to Arjuna that wise men do not worry when they leave one body to take another.

Similarly, at the moment of death there is also no extinction of the individuality. The embodied ego of the dead body leaves its previous form, and according to the *vāsanās* (mental impressions) that it gathered during its embodiment, becomes identi-fied with particular physical equipment so that it can express itself completely and seek its fulfillment.

The Self Is Eternal

Therefore, our endeavor should be to rediscover the one vital Power on which this panorama of life is recorded. To find It is to realize the supreme Truth, and should be the main purpose of our lives. What we now understand as real (*sat*) is really unreal (*asat*) and as such has no being:

> *The unreal has no being; there is no nonbeing of the Real; the truth about both these has been seen by the knowers of the Truth (or the seers of the Essence).* (II:16)

Only a few people have fathomed the depth of this truth and to them the vagaries of life and the varieties of experiences hold no value at all. The really wise person is one who has intellectually grasped this truth about life. Yet, there is the one vital Power, pervading everything, which is the very substance of all the worlds of perceptions, which is indestructible.

> *Know That to be indestructible by which all this is pervaded. None can cause the destruction of That—the Imperishable.* (II:17)

These bodies of the embodied Self are perishable, indeed, and the only factor that is indestructible in this multiplicity is the pure, indestructible Ātman.

> *They have an end, it is said, these bodies of the embodied Self. The Self is Eternal, Indestructible, Incomprehensible. Therefore fight, O Bharata.* (II:18)

And that Indweller in this physical equipment is not born, nor does He ever die.

> *He is not born, nor does He ever die; after having been, He again ceases not to be; Unborn, Eternal, Changeless, and Ancient, He is not killed when the body is killed.* (II:20)

Having thus made it clear that the Self is neither an agent, nor an object of the action of slaying, and having established the immutability of the Self, Krishna sums up the argument by saying:

> *Whosoever knows Him to be Indestructible, Eternal, Unborn, and Inexhaustible, how can that man slay, O Partha, or cause others to be slain.* (II:21)

Weapons cleave It not, and fire burns It not, water wets It not, and wind dries It not. This Self cannot be cut, nor burnt, nor moistened, nor dried up. It is Eternal, All-pervading, Stable, Immovable, and Ancient. This Self is said to be Unmanifest, Unthinkable, and Unchangeable. Therefore, knowing this to be such, you should not grieve. (II:23-25)

Caught as it were in the whirlpool of change, this eternal Self goes on changing one embodiment after another.

Just as a man casts off his worn-out clothes and puts on new ones, so also the embodied self casts off its worn-out bodies and enters others that are new. (II:22)

Old bodies may die, and new bodies may be taken up, but there is no occasion to moan over this inevitable change. But if you think of Him as constantly born and constantly dying, even then, O mighty-armed, you should not grieve.

Indeed, certain is death for the born, and certain is birth for the dead; therefore, you should not grieve over the inevitable. (II:27)

Birth and death have to follow each other systematically to keep up the balance in nature. To weep over death is stupidity indeed. Like the woman in the Buddhist fable, we are also deluded that death and sorrow are misfortunes affecting our individual selves. Calm reasoning is needed to pull us out of this muddle of vain sorrows, and to surrender wholeheartedly to this universal law in a spirit of reverence and gratitude.

IX

Consecrated Living

by Swami Paramananda

Our present life well-lived gives us power over the life that is to come. Therefore, wise men regard their life as a sacred gift—not something that has come by chance and which can be used for their own gratification. It does not rise and set with this physical span of existence. They know that this body is nothing but a garment, which they change when its usefulness is over. It is wrong, therefore, to cling to it, for when this one is worn out, the soul takes another that is better suited for its further evolution. Death may bring a lull, a brief interruption, but those who are already alive in a spiritual sense, they go onward and forward without delay. It is only those who are in slumber spiritually, though they may appear to be physically awake, who find the gulf very wide.

In our life, therefore, we must prepare ourselves for the life beyond. If our thoughts and ambitions are saturated with vulgar material concerns, can we suddenly appreciate something fine and lofty? Can we suddenly become unselfish? Can we suddenly become holy? It is through the habits of our present life that we acquire these qualities. We must make ourselves ready for what comes hereafter by utilizing wisely all the opportunities given to us in this life. Through the actions that we perform with diligence, simplicity, selfless devotion, and consecration, we build a bridge. The bridge that will hold us securely when we cross, but it must be done by ourselves. Priests, ministers, and spiritual teachers can give us hints of what we should do, they may inspire us and stimulate us, but this age-old problem comes to each soul afresh and each must meet it individually.

We must meet it bravely. We must prove our worth every instant—not only in big things, but also in small things. It is not merely our hours of prayer, but quite as much our hours of activity that determine our merit. Our prayer becomes useless when our activity is not in harmony with it. Our spiritual life and our worldly life should go together in perfect unison. This is a great lesson that we learn from the rishis. They put very little emphasis on the form of religion that an individual follows. Each soul has to deal with God directly they say. A child always goes to its mother. In all circumstances—in sorrow, in happiness—there cannot be any separation, unless the child forgets and forsakes the mother. Misled by the glamour of the material world, how often we forget our relation with our divine Parent, but this should not be. We do not love our fellow-beings less if we love God with our whole heart and soul. On the contrary, the love we give is richer and nobler.

Gaining a Larger Viewpoint

Life is never irksome or arduous when we gain this larger viewpoint. We are no longer afraid of living, nor are we afraid of dying. All fear springs from the narrow side of our nature. Egotism, selfish greed, and ignorance create fear. The large-minded, selfless man is never afraid. There can be no fear in our hearts except when we are selfish. If a person walks with God and feels his heart as part of God's heart, nothing can frighten him. There are certain orthodox teachings that declare it to be sacrilegious to claim that we are a part of the divine, but did not Christ teach this? Did he not say: "Be ye perfect even as your Father which is in heaven is perfect!"

Also, in the Upanishads we read: "Thou art That"; thou art in essence one with infinite and unalterable Being. Is this not the theme echoing through all spiritual teachings—that unless we become Godlike, we cannot enter into conscious union with God. Unless we become truly alive, we cannot conquer death?

We all have the power to conquer death, but not in the physical sense. The material person would like to prolong his earthly life indefinitely. That is not possible. The combination of material elements that make up this physical body must dissolve eventually, but within this combination there is something finer, less destructible—the causal body, which will outlast this gross body. Our thoughts and aspirations, desires and feelings, our thirst for material things and our yearning for the spiritual, are all contained in this, and according to the measure of the spiritual or the material we do obtain what we deserve. Our future destiny is wholly molded by ourselves. You may ask, If we mold our own destiny, what does God do? But even granted that He molds it, we still supply the material out of which He shapes it. He is not an arbitrary, partial revengeful deity.

Our life is full of opportunities through which we may secure progress and freedom. If we do not take advantage of these opportunities, it is our own misfortune. But nothing is lasting and we can always eradicate our failures. What we make we have the power to unmake. There is no mistake so terrible that it will overthrow the soul and condemn it to eternal perdition. Could an all-wise, all-loving Providence condemn any child of His to everlasting suffering? He grants us another life, another opportunity, another advantage, so that we may still prove our worth and work out our salvation. So we must keep on. We must work to purify ourselves, to sanctify and uplift ourselves, so that we may escape from the bondage of ignorance.

God gives us ample time and opportunity. There is no reason to be anxious or hasty. In our modern life this constant nervous haste is one of the greatest drawbacks to spiritual progress. Man takes his life too hurriedly. Before he has formulated his ideas, he begins to act. As a result, his actions bring him bondage and must be undone to release him from that bondage. Let us cultivate a calmer, broader view of life. Through greater spiritual understanding, let us try to realize that our soul is not the thing of one day. The body may rise and fall, but the soul is eternal and immortal. "Swords cannot pierce it, fire cannot burn it, water cannot wet it, air cannot dry it." This is the nature of the soul that dwells within this body.

A materialist claims that this is not true. He says, swords can pierce me, and the wise man says, they cannot. Thus, they are constantly at odds. Where does this conflict come from? It rises from the fact that one is looking without, and the other is looking within. The one is dependent on material existence and the other on spiritual existence, but the conflict cannot last.

The individual who now insists, "I am this body, I am Mr. So and So," will some day throw off the shackles of ignorance and rise into the knowledge of his true Being. This is the real resurrection—when we can rise out of the grave of ignorance and materialism. Life does not hold much joy for us if we are constantly fearful, driven by selfish desires, and constantly overwhelmed by physical consciousness. Real joy comes when we have a new and bigger vision. For one who has gained that, the gulf between life here and hereafter is destroyed.

To Know and to Become

Through devotion to God and service to our fellow beings, we prepare ourselves to pass from this life to that other, and our mind learns to dwell habitually on our Ideal. Lord Krishna tells us in the *Bhagavad Gītā* that what we think upon at the time of our bodily death decides our next state in evolution. Therefore, He admonishes us at all times to think of the Supreme and do our work faithfully, for if our mind and intellect are wholly dedicated to Him, we shall no doubt attain unto Him. But if our last thought molds our destiny, then all we have to do, it would seem, is to make our last thought a perfect one. Can we do it? One who is striving for perfection now can hold a perfect thought at the moment of passing. Can a person suddenly think of something high and lofty? Can he suddenly paint a master-piece? He strives for it. He thinks, he dreams, he imagines, his whole being is on fire with it, and that fire consumes his limita-tions and he can paint a great picture. So it is with us when our whole being is on fire with spiritual yearning. That fire burns off the blemishes of our nature and lofty thoughts become habitual with us.

Did our life begin with this bodily existence? That is not possible, for something cannot come out of nothing. Like a tree, it must spring from a seed sown somewhere. The feelings and tendencies and aspirations that we possess here must have had their origin in some previous state. They must be the result of past experiences and effort. You may ask, who keeps the record of our past? But do not imagine that an invisible Providence keeps a record and decides our reward and punishment. It is we ourselves who keep the record. Every selfish and every loving thought, every good or bad deed is stored up in our own charac-ter and condition of life, and we receive the fruits of these.

Life offers us innumerable opportunities. We cannot com-plain that we lack them. We are placed just where we can ad-vance most quickly. We may not believe it, and we may think that someone else has a better chance than we have, but the all-wise One knows what is best suited for each. And if we have true longing and love for the Ideal, we shall take the material placed in our hands and out of it mold a beautiful life. The lesson we have to learn is not how we can get better opportunities, but how we may make the best use of those we have. We take our place according to our merit. No one can force us to take any other place than the one we deserve. We cannot stay where we do not belong. Even if someone should put us in a perfect region, we would find ourselves out of place there. We would not know how to speak the language of that region, nor would we be able to enjoy the freedom it might offer us.

Living life in harmony with a spiritual ideal alone will enable us to benefit by the privileges of a higher sphere. All that is asked of us is to do our daily tasks with a prayerful and consecrated attitude of mind. Then whatever the hereafter may owe us will be given to us. It is better to ask nothing, because we cannot ask wisely. But we can do each thing with humility, with surrender and with the prayer "Thy will be done." When we do this, we are safe. Our human side always blunders, but this human side can be brought into such absolute harmony with the Divine that it will become permeated with Divine Life and move in rhythm with it.

Within us is immortal life. When we know that, how can we fear death? Our consciousness must be trained to dwell on the immortal part in us. That is the only way to conquer the afflictions of this mortal life. Until we possess the Knowledge of our immortal nature, nothing can relieve us permanently from the fears and miseries that confront us. To know and to become— these alone will enable us to enter that other life with perfect peace and freedom.

X

The Good News

by Anthony de Mello

I imagine that I have a few days left of life.
I am allowed to choose just one person,
or at the most two,
to be with me for these last days.
I make the painful choice,
then I talk with this person,
explaining why it is I chose him or her.

I am allowed to have
a three-minute conversation on the phone
with any person of my choice
or to send each one of them a written message.
Whom do I choose?
What do I say?
What does each of them reply?

I have a final chance
to reach out to people I disliked
or people I ignored.
If I take it, what do I say to each of them
now that I feel myself to be
on the threshold of eternity?

ANTHONY DE MELLO

People ask me if I have a final wish.
Have I?

A friend tells me he plans to speak
at my memorial service.
I suggest a point or two
for him to put into his speech.

One day, alone in my room,
I think of the things in my life
I am especially thankful for,
the things that I am proud of.

Then I turn to the things I regret
and wish had never happened,
especially my sins.

While I am thus engaged, Jesus Christ walks in.
His presence brings the sweetest joy and peace.
I tell Him some of the things about my life that I regret.
He stops me with the words,
"That is all forgiven and forgotten.
Do you not know
that love keeps no record of wrongs?" (I Cor. 13:5)
Then He goes on to say,
"In fact, your wrongs have not just been forgiven.
They have even been converted into grace.
Have you never been told
that where the sin was great,
grace was greater still?" (Rom. 5:21)

This seems too good to be true
for my poor fearful heart!
Then I hear Him say, "I am so pleased with you,
so grateful to you."

I begin to protest that there is nothing in my life
that He can be so pleased about or grateful for.
He says, "Surely you would be grateful beyond words
to anyone who did for you
even a small part of what you did for Me?
Do you think I have less of a heart than you?"
So I lean back
and allow the impact of His words to hit me,
rejoicing in my heart
that I have such a God as He.

PART THREE

Teachings for Life and Death

*The work of philosophy
results in liberation
from the fear of death.*

Paul Brunton

The Soul is God. It alone is Truth. It is without a second. It is what gives life to the body, the senses, and the mind. Like the sky it exists everywhere and in everything. It is unlimited by time and space. It is self-luminous and the embodiment of Knowledge, Existence, and Bliss. No one can deny It. The most careful observation of natural laws, the speediest progress of science, the newest and the most valuable discoveries; not one of these can reject the existence of God. On careful thought we can see that the discoveries of natural science only prove and not disprove the existence of the Soul. If anyone thinks otherwise, it is nothing but his folly.

That I am not this inert, earth-like, mass of flesh of five or six feet, but the Soul, the embodiment of life, is a truth that can never perish. It was so in the past, it is so in the present, and it will be so in the future. Remember this: Even when this body composed of the five elements decomposes, the life that illuminates it and activates it, never perishes. That life is the Soul. That Soul is you. Believe this firmly. Detach yourself from this body which may perish today or tomorrow; believe in the immortal Soul and acquire soul-force and thereby bless yourself, bless others, bless the world and reclaim it from all disability. May you become bejeweled beacons of inextinguishable spiritual light!

Swami Tapovanam
Wanderings in the Himalayas

XI

The Five Strengths

by Pema Chödrön

The five strengths are the subject of two slogans:
> Practice the five strengths,
> The condensed heart instructions.
> The mahayana instruction for ejection of consciousness
> at death is the five strengths:
> How you conduct yourself is important.[1]

The underlying point of all our study and practice is that the happiness we seek is here to connect with at any time. The happiness we seek is our birthright. To discover it we need to be more gentle with ourselves, more compassionate toward ourselves and our universe. The happiness we seek cannot be found through grasping, trying to hold on to things. It cannot be found through getting serious and uptight about wanting things to go in the direction that we think will bring happiness. We are always taking hold of the wrong end of the stick. The point is that the happiness we seek is already here and it will be found through relaxation and letting go rather than through struggle.

Does that mean you can just sleep all day? Does that mean there is nothing you need to do? The answer is no. There does seem to be something that we have to do. These slogans tell us to practice the five strengths: strong determination, familiarization, seed of virtue, reproach, and aspiration. The five strengths are five sources of inspiration to trust that we have got all that we need in the palm of our hand.

These are the heart instructions on how to live and how to die. Last year I spent some time with two people who were dying. Jack and Jill were both old friends; they each had a very different relationship with their death. They each had the privilege of knowing quite a few months in advance that they were going to die, which is a great gift. Both of them began to fade away. When things began to slip away on Jack, when his body stopped working well for him, he was angry at the beginning, but then something started to shift, and he began to relax. When it was clear that everything was dissolving and slipping away, he seemed to get happier and happier. It felt as if he were letting go of all the things that had kept him separate from his basic goodness, letting everything go. He would say things like, "There is nothing to do, there is nothing to want," and he would start to laugh. Day by day he wasted away more, but that was not a fundamental problem; this dissolving was very liberating for him.

The external situation was the same for Jill, but she got scared, and she began to struggle against the whole process. As her body started to waste away and there was less to hold on to, she became more grim and terrified, clenching her teeth and her hands. She was facing a vast abyss and was going to be pushed over into it, and she was screaming with terror, "No! No! No!"

The Way to Live

I understood why I practice: we can discover the process of letting go and relaxing during our lifetime. In fact, that is the way to live: stop struggling against the fact that things are slipping through our fingers. Stop struggling against the fact that nothing is solid to begin with and things do not last. Knowing that can give us a lot of space and a lot of room if we can relax with it instead of screaming and struggling against it.

The five strengths are instructions on how to live and how to die. Actually, there is no difference. The same good advice applies to both, because if you know how to die then you know how to live and if you know how to live then you will know how to die. Suzuki Roshi said, "Just be willing to die over and over again." As each breath goes out, let it be the end of that moment and the birth of something new. All those thoughts, as they come up, just see them and let them go, let the whole story line die; let the space for something new arise. The five strengths address how to give up trying all the time to grasp what is ungraspable and actually relax into the space that is there. Then what do we find? Maybe that is the point. We are afraid to find out.

Strong Determination

The first strength is strong determination. Rather than some kind of dogged pushing through, strong determination involves connecting with joy, relaxing, and trusting. It is determination to use every challenge you meet as an opportunity to open your heart and soften, determination not to withdraw. One simple way to develop this strength is to develop a strong-hearted spiritual appetite. To do this, some kind of playful quality is needed. When you wake up in the morning, you can say, "I wonder what is going to happen today. This may be the day that I die. This may be the day that I understand what all these teachings are about." The Native Americans, before they went into battle, would say, "Today is a good day to die." You could also say, "Today is a good day to live."

Strong determination gives you the vehicle that you need to find out for yourself that you have everything it takes, that the fundamental happiness is right here, waiting. Strong determination not to shut anything out of your heart and not to close up takes a sense of humor and an appetite, an appetite for enlightenment.

Familiarization

The next strength is familiarization. What familiarization means is that the dharma no longer feels like a foreign entity: your first thought becomes dharmic. You begin to realize that all the teachings are about yourself; you're here to study yourself. Dharma isn't philosophy. Dharma is basically a good recipe for how to cook yourself, how to soften the hardest, toughest piece of meat. Dharma is good instruction on how to stop cheating yourself, how to stop robbing yourself, how to find out who you really are, not in the limited sense of "I need" and "I am gonna get," but through developing wakefulness as your habit, your way of perceiving everything.

We talk about enlightenment as if it is a big accomplishment. Basically, it has to do with relaxing and finding out what you already have. The enlightened "you" might be a slightly different "you" from the one you are familiar with, but it still has hair growing out of its head, still has taste buds, and when it gets the flu, snot comes out of its nose. Enlightened, however, you might experience yourself in a slightly less claustrophobic way, maybe a completely nonclaustrophobic way.

Familiarization means that you do not have to search any further, and you know it. It is all in the "pleasantness of the presentness," in the very discursive thoughts you are having now, in all the emotions that are coursing through you; it is all in there somehow.

The Seed of Virtue

The third strength is called the seed of virtue. In effect, this is Buddha nature or basic goodness. It's like a swimming pool with no sides that you are swimming in forever. In fact, you are made out of water. Buddha nature is not like a heart transplant that you get from elsewhere. "It is not as if you are trying to teach a tree to talk," as Rinpoche once said. It is just something that can be awakened or, you might say, relaxed into. Let yourself fall apart into wakefulness. The strength comes from the fact that the seed is already there; with warmth and moisture it sprouts and becomes visible above the ground. You find yourself looking like a daffodil, or feeling like one, anyway. The practice is about softening or relaxing, but it is also about precision and seeing clearly. None of that implies searching. Searching for happiness prevents us from ever finding it.

Reproach

The fourth strength is called reproach. This one requires talking to yourself: "Ego, you have done nothing but cause me problems for ages. Give me a break. I am not buying it anymore." Try it in the shower. You should talk to yourself all the time without embarrassment. When you see yourself starting to spin off in frivolity, say to yourself, "Begone, you troublemaker!"

This approach can be slightly problematic because we do not usually distinguish between who we think we are and our ego. The more gentleness that comes up, the more friendliness you feel for yourself, the more this dialogue is fruitful. But to the degree that you actually are hard on yourself, then this dialogue could just increase your self-criticism.

Over the years, with encouragement from wonderful teachers, I have found that, rather than blaming yourself or yelling at yourself, you can teach the dharma to yourself. Reproach does not have to be a negative reaction to your personal brand of insanity. But it does imply that you see insanity as insanity, neurosis as neurosis, spinning off as spinning off. At that point, you can teach the dharma to yourself.

This advice was given to me by Thrangu Rinpoche. I was having anxiety attacks, and he said that I should teach the dharma to myself, just good simple dharma. So now I say, "Pema, what do you really want? Do you want to shut down and close off, do you want to stay imprisoned? Or do you want to let yourself relax here, let yourself die? Here is your chance to actually realize something. Here is your chance not to be stuck. So what do you really want? Do you want always to be right or do you want to wake up?"

Reproach can be very powerful. You yourself teach yourself the dharma in your own words. You can teach yourself the four noble truths, you can teach yourself about taking refuge—anything that has to do with that moment when you are just about to recreate *samsāra* (the vicious cycle of existence) as if you personally had invented it. Look ahead to the rest of your life and ask yourself what you want it to add up to.

Each time you are willing to see your thoughts as empty, let them go, and come back to your breath, you are sowing seeds of wakefulness, seeds of being able to see the nature of mind, and seeds of being able to rest in unconditional space. It does not matter that you cannot do it every time. Just the willingness, the strong determination to do it, is sowing the seeds of virtue. You find that you can do it more spontaneously and naturally, without it being an effort. It begins with some sense of exertion and becomes your normal state. That is the seed of *bodhicitta* ("awakened heart" or "courageous heart") ripening. You find out who you really are.

Aspiration

The last strength, aspiration, is also a powerful tool. A heartfelt sense of aspiring cuts through negativity about yourself; it cuts through the heavy trips you lay on yourself. The notion of aspiration is simply that you voice your wishes for enlightenment. You say to yourself, for yourself, about yourself, and by yourself, things like, "May my compassion for myself increase." You might be feeling completely hopeless, down on yourself, and you can voice your heartfelt aspiration: "May my sense of being obstructed decrease. May my experience of wakefulness increase. May I experience my fundamental wisdom. May I think of others before myself."

Aspiration is much like prayer, except that there is nobody who hears you.

Aspiration, yet again, is to talk to yourself, to be an eccentric *bodhisattva*. It is a way to empower yourself. In fact, all five of these strengths are ways to empower yourself. Buddhism itself is all about empowering yourself, not about getting what you want.

The five strengths are the heart instructions on how to live and how to die. Whether it is right now or at the moment of your death, they tell you how to wake up to whatever is going on.

FOOTNOTE:

[1] Point Four: From *The Root Text of the Seven Points of Training the Mind*, by Chekawa Yeshe Dorje.

XII

Ego and the True Self

by Swami Abhedananda

[*The following article is from* Mystery of Death. *The* Katha Upaniṣad *discourses recorded in this book were given as lectures by Swami Abhedananda before audiences in North America in 1906.*]

Whenever we try to study the mystery of death, we are confronted with various questions: What is the true nature of our being? What is soul life? Is the soul life eternal or not? What is the relation of the ego to the universe? What are ego and true Self? These are some important questions that face us in our pursuit of the mystery of death. The right solution of these vital questions gives us knowledge about what happens after death.

Therefore, in the *Katha Upaniṣad,* Yama, the Ruler of Death, while describing the relation of the individual ego to God said: "Two have entered into the cave of the heart, dwelling on the summit of the spiritual space."[1]

The seers of Truth say that the one is like the self-effulgent sun, the other is like his image or reflection. The one is like the witness, while the other eats the fruits of its own thoughts and deeds. It is tremendously difficult to clearly grasp this vital point. Many thinking minds have often been deluded in trying to grasp this most subtle subject, therefore, there is a bewildering diversity of opinions on this issue. The idea that is common to Christianity is that God created man in His own image. . . . But minds that can grasp the real meaning of the word "image" are very rare. It is said that man is created in the image of God. Here "man" stands for all human beings. The reference is not to the human body, because the human body is not always perfect, in fact, it has many limitations. Therefore, if the imperfect human body was created in the image of God, then God also must share all those imperfections in common with the creation. The image is a reflection of the original. It is for this and various other reasons we cannot think that the human form alone is referred to by the word "image." On the contrary, the word "image" refers to "ego" or the "soul". . . .

Students of Vedanta can easily grasp the meaning because they do not think of a human God when they try to explain the word *image*. The individual soul, the *jīva*, is the image of God, who is the Spirit. He is the universal Spirit. He is like the self-effulgent sun, and each individual soul is like a reflection of the sun on the mirror of the intellect. As the reflection cannot exist without being related to the object of reflection, similarly the individual soul cannot exist without being closely related to the Being, the Spirit, whose reflection it is.

If you hold a mirror in the sun you will see the reflection, but that reflection would be impossible if there was no sun, or if the sun was covered by dense clouds. The reflection is only possible when there is sun overhead. If we are the reflections or images of God, then we must be of similar nature, because the reflection of the sun cannot be square or triangular, but round, self-effulgent, and bright. That is our true nature if we are created in the image of God. If we are created in His image then we are also bright and we are spirits.

But where is that self-effulgent sun, the Being, God, whose reflections the individual souls are? He is not very far from us; He is within us, around us, though He is not visible to the eyes. Sense powers cannot reveal His presence. The materialistic thinkers and scientists try to understand God through sense powers. And when they fail, they deny His existence, but they never think for a moment that the sense powers exist in and through God, but cannot reveal God. The individual souls, also, cannot be revealed by sense powers. Only the manifestation of certain activities can be perceived by the senses and that is all.

You cannot tell whether there is a soul in another person or not, but you can conceive that a person is alive when he moves, talks, or does certain things. You can guess and infer by observing certain acts, but the Reality, the real nature, cannot be perceived by our senses. Unless the egos assume certain forms they cannot be perceived by our senses.

Now we have understood the relation between God and the individual ego. God Himself is sexless. He is both father and mother of the universe, and if He is sexless, the individual soul is also sexless. . . . Sex conditions are more or less related to the body and the mind, but not to the soul. The soul is higher than sex. There is no masculine or feminine soul; every one is a child of God.

The Mediator

The individual soul is to be considered as a nexus, the link between the world of senses and the realm of the Absolute, it is like a bridge. If we wish to go to the realm of the Absolute, we must go over that bridge, and, therefore, the individual soul is called the mediator—the bridge. The Christians call it Christ. Christ means the individual soul, the ego, which is the mediator, which connects the phenomenal world with the Absolute. We cannot go to the realm of Divinity by any other way except over the bridge of our souls. Therefore, if you wish to know God, first know yourself. That is the surest way. If you wish to know Christ, know yourself, and there you will find Christ.

Christ does not mean an ordinary human being; it refers to a child of God. We are all children of God, and when we realize that truth we will realize Christ. The historical Christ is limited by time and place, but the spiritual Christ is above time and place, and eternal by nature. The spiritual Christ dwells in every individual soul from the beginningless past and is the real Christ. He is the mediator, and he signifies the individual soul in man. The soul is eternal and immortal. But we cannot attain to immortality unless we have gone over the bridge of our own souls; that alone can lead us to the abode of immortality. Let us now understand the nature of this bridge, the mediator between the mortal and immortal.

We can grasp the nature of our soul only by means of analysis, by studying our own self and by understanding our own being. No one can give us that supreme Knowledge. External teachers may give you certain suggestions, but each individual must find out for himself where the soul is and what it is like. It is a difficult task, yet it must be courageously undertaken. It is difficult when we are lazy, or living on the sense plane, because we are then deluded by false thinking, and since we are sleeping in self-delusion, it is difficult to get it. But if we are awakened, if we have a genuine longing for the Truth, to realize God, it is easily achieved.

People who say, "Oh, we are so busy, we have to do so many things, and we have no time to think of ourselves, or to think of God" are deluding themselves and wasting their energy fruitlessly. They are only working for their bread and butter and a little sense pleasure. After a hard day's work they go to bed, and after waking up they go back to work again. This round of working and sleeping, eating and drinking, goes on repeatedly. There is no rest. They neglect their own selves. They do not open their eyes and do not know anything beyond a certain limit. Observe how they are living and what they are doing, how foolish people are to waste their time and energy on things that do not amount to anything, things that do not bring any consolation or happiness, no knowledge of their own Self, or knowledge of their relationship to God.

The Analogy of the Chariot

To analyze ourselves and to find out the relation between the senses, mind, intellect, and our own selves, the egos, we can use the analogy of the chariot as an illustration. Here the Ruler of Death gives the following illustration that may help seekers after Truth:

> Consider this body as a chariot. The rider or master is the soul; the horses are the senses, that is, the sense organs and sense powers are the horses. The driver is the intellect, and the mind the reins. The objects of the senses are the roads where these horses are traveling or running. Form a picture of that in your mind, your body like a chariot, but your true Self as the Master, and the horses are the sense powers going in different directions. Then you can understand the relation between the senses, sense powers, mind, intellect, and your conscious ego and how they exist, and what relations they bear to each other.[2]

In the above analogy, if the master or rider is our true Self, which is called Ātman in Sanskrit, who is the eternal and immortal part of our own self, and the prime mover of our thoughts and actions, then the rider is above and beyond all imperfections. It is not affected by sensations of pleasure or pain, but the ego is affected. The thinker, the doer, the knower of pain is not the true Self, but it is the thinking, eating, drinking, planning, and working person. It is the ego imbued with I-consciousness. But behind this ego you will find the rider, the true Self. This ego is a combination of the true Self, the intellect, the mind, and sense powers. It is all combined. When all these different powers are fused into a whole, that whole is the ordinary ego. The ordinary man or woman who thinks I am the son or daughter of Mr. So and So, I have my children, family, or work to do is the mortal ego. But the mortal man is in reality an immortal entity. Or it can be said that the immortal entity forms the background of the mortal man or ego, who thinks and feels.

In this chariot, the driver is responsible for every good and evil performed. If the driver is not careful, the horses will drag the chariot down into the ditch. The horses are very powerful. The horses will become unruly if the driver is not strong. If the driver does not know how to manage all these horses, the ego will suffer. On the other hand, if the driver knows the right path and the right way by which he can manage the horses, there will be no suffering. A person who is dull of understanding, whose mind is unbridled, naturally cannot control the horses or his senses. You can now see how an ordinary person, who is under the influence of sense powers, cannot control the horses because the driver is not strong. When he does not have proper understanding and enough self-control, the horses get the upper hand and drag the driver, willing or unwilling, in any direction they desire.

You will find the vast majority of people have no control over their horses. Many people while looking at shop windows are attracted by objects that they want to possess immediately. If they have no money, they will even steal things and all kinds of trouble follows. That is the attraction of the power of seeing. The sight of an object produces such strong impressions. And when the driver does not possess understanding and self-control, they all go into the ditch. If such persons had some self-control and exercised proper reasoning in dissuading themselves from the mad pursuit of the objects of allurement, they could avoid many troubles.

Conditions for Reaching Perfection

One who has right understanding, whose mind is always firmly held, holds all the horses together. That driver holds the reins of the power of attention. He whose mind is always firmly held has his senses under control like the good horses of a charioteer. The horses obey such a driver. But if the horses know that the driver is not strong, the horses will take their own course.

Therefore, if the horses of our chariot—our senses—find that the driver is not firm, the rein is not tight, they go astray and do whatever they please. Let us all remember this illustration. It is very helpful. If you can hold the reins of the mind firmly, and use the powers of discrimination and understanding properly, you will have no trouble, no matter where you go in the world.

There is another thing to be considered: If we are not mindful of our own self, of our own duties, and if we are impure in our thoughts and ideas, we cannot attain to perfection. To achieve perfection we must first purify ourselves, purify our minds, purify our senses, exercise self-control, and use discrimination. Understand the moral, mental, physical, and spiritual laws properly and live up to those laws.

Most people are without discrimination. But if you can discriminate between what is right and wrong you can get rid of lots of trouble. Right discrimination is the highest guide in this world. A person who lacks discrimination lives quite naturally in the darkness of ignorance and consequently suffers endless pains and miseries in life.

If you walk on the street one wintery morning just looking up at the clouds and ignoring the slippery ground, you are bound to fall and break your neck. You must exercise the powers of attention and discrimination. Be mindful of these two things in your day-to-day life and also in the performance of your duties. Pure thoughts and ideas must be held as pure friends as you use discrimination. Impure thoughts and ideas will lead us into misery, and are never helpful. To purify our inner nature we must cherish holy thoughts in our minds. Everything that is uplifting, everything that is beneficial to humankind, everything that makes us unselfish, everything that makes us forget ourselves, everything that helps us in cultivating conscious self-denial, is the ideal of life. Every time we deny ourselves we grow, the more we give, the more we receive. We deny ourselves every time we give something to another person whose need is greater than ours, instead of keeping it for ourselves.

Instead of holding impure thoughts of possessiveness, we must hold thoughts of truthfulness. No matter how often we may be cheated or robbed, we should never cheat or rob others. Make that a firm resolution; that you shall never do any wrong to anyone no matter how you may be injured or hurt, and that would be your principle under all conditions. If you starve, you should not sacrifice your principle, but sacrifice your body rather than your principle. That kind of firmness is necessary. If children are taught these ideas from early childhood and trained to deny themselves, they will become Christlike. There would be no need of police, and no need of state laws if individuals lived in this way.

He who has right knowledge, who has self-control, who is pure, reaches perfection and lasting bliss. These are the conditions of reaching perfection. First, we must have true knowledge, right discrimination between the eternal and noneternal, spirit and matter, the soul and body, and right and wrong. All these things we must know as they are in reality. If we have that knowledge, if we can distinguish the soul from the body, spirit from matter, and right from wrong, then, with the help of that knowledge we can attain to perfection.

Affirm the Highest

At the same time we must have self-control, hold the reins of the senses in check and we must not allow the horses to drag us into the ditch of despair, sorrow, suffering, and misery. Exercise self-control at every moment of your life. If any passion arises, deny it instead of encouraging it. Deny all the passions, saying, "I have no passion. I am the highest." Every time anything attracts you, deny it. Try self-denial and you will find that you have risen above the level of ordinary mortals. What can be more practical than this? We can practice this always, when we are alone, or when we are with our friends and relatives. When we practice self-denial, we shall find that everybody will appreciate it in the end. Those who deny themselves in social life are always respected and honored.

The greatest philanthropists denied themselves. That is the sure way to prosperity, godliness, righteousness, and spirituality. With the help of that self-control and right knowledge we can reach perfection in the end. Then we shall know what is meant by perfection. Now we may cherish odd ideas about it. We think that perfection means a kind of heaven where we get all kinds of enjoyment without suffering and misery. That is an idea that some people cherish, but that is a wrong conception. Heavenly bliss is not equivalent to the state of perfection.

Very few people know what is meant by perfection. Perfection means a state in which all your senses and passions are under control and you are the absolute master of your own self. Perfection does not mean a realm, but a state of existence, a level of enlarged consciousness where we come in tune with the Infinite. Christ had attained to that state and therefore He was perfect. Omniscience will mark that stage. In the state of perfection your past, present, and future will be equally revealed to you in their fullness. Everything will then open to you. You will then understand all the laws, gross or subtle, which govern physical, mental, and spiritual planes. You will then understand your true nature and its relation to the infinite Being. All vital questions like the nature of the infinite Being, Its source and history, and the roots of all phenomena will be solved at that stage. We are capable of that great achievement. That should be our ideal, not eating, drinking, and earning money.

Three conditions are essential for achieving the highest end in life. These are self-control, self-denial, and right knowledge; any person who possesses these three will attain to the highest goal of all religions. Whether you believe in God or not, you will attain to God, which signifies perfection, if you simply possess these three great qualities. Belief in God is not necessary for salvation. Belief is an accompaniment of right knowledge. Knowledge and belief spring simultaneously. Blind faith does not help us in any way. Only that belief is helpful which is fed and kindled by right knowledge and discrimination. That faith, once acquired, is unshakable. It cannot be changed; it is indestructible.

FOOTNOTES:

[1] *Katha Upaniṣad,* Section III: 1.
[2] *Katha Upaniṣad,* Section III: 3,4.

XIII

Conversations on Conscious Immortality with Ramana Maharshi

Recorded by Paul Brunton and Munagala Venkataramiah

Q: We grieve when a person whom we love dies. Shall we avoid such grief by either loving all alike or by not loving at all?

A: If one person dies there is grief for the other person who still lives. The way to get rid of grief is not to live. Kill the one who grieves. Who will then remain to suffer? The ego must die. That is the only way. The two alternatives amount to the same state. When all is the Self, who is there to be loved or hated?

There is a class of people who want to know all about the future and past births, but they ignore the present. The load from the past is the present misery. Why recall the past, it is a waste of time.

The Self is the electric dynamo, the mind is the contact switchboard, while the body is the lamp. When the karma hour comes to give death, the mind switches off the current and withdraws the light-life from the body. Both mind and vitality are manifestations of the supreme life force, the Self.

Q: What happens to an individual after death?

A: Engage yourself in the living present. The future will

take care of itself. Do not worry about the future. The state before creation and the process of creation are dealt with in the scriptures in order that you may know the present. Because you say you are born, therefore they talk about it.

What is birth? Is it of the "I-thought" or of the body? Is "I" separate from the body or identical? How did this "I-thought" arise? Is the "I-thought" your nature? Or is something else your nature?

The "I" of the wise man includes the body but he does not identify himself with the body. For there cannot be anything apart from "I" for him. If the body falls, there is no loss for the "I." "I" remains the same. If the body feels dead, let it raise the question. Being inert, it cannot. "I" never dies and does not ask. Who then dies? Who asks?

Q: From where does the ego rise?

A: Soul, mind, ego are mere words. There are no true entities of the kind. Consciousness is the only truth. Forgetfulness of your real nature is the real death; remembrance of it is the true birth. It puts an end to successive births. Yours is the eternal life. How does the desire for eternal life arise? Because the present state is unbearable. Why? Because it is not your true nature. Had it been your real nature, there would be no desire to agitate you. How does the present state differ from your real nature? You are spirit in truth.

Troubles arise because we consider ourselves limited. The idea is wrong. In sleep there was no world, no ego, and no trouble. Something wakes up from that happy state and says "I." To that ego the world appears. It is the rise of the ego that is the cause of the trouble. Let him trace the ego to its source and he will reach that undifferentiated Source, a state that is sleepless sleep. The Self is ever there; wisdom only appears to dawn, though it is but natural.

Q: Are ego and Self the same?

A: Self can be without the ego, but the ego cannot be without the Self. Egos are like bubbles in the ocean. Impurities and worldly attachments affect only the ego; the Self remains pure and unaffected. All these are only mental concepts. You are now identifying yourself with a wrong "I" which is the "I-thought." This "I-thought" rises and sinks whereas the true significance of "I" cannot do so. There cannot be a break in your being. The father of your personal "I" is the real "I," God. Try to find out the source of the individual "I" and then you will reach the other "I." When the individual goes, the desires also go.

True Self-Reliance

Q: I was once very self-reliant. I fear in old age that people will laugh at me.

A: Even when you said you were self-reliant, it was not so—you were ego-reliant. Instead of this, if you let go of ego, you will get real Self-reliance. Your pride was merely pride of ego. As long as you identify yourself with the ego, you will recognize others as individuals also, then there is room for pride. Let that drop and you drop others' ego as well and so there is no more room for pride. As long as there is the sense of separation, there will be afflicting thoughts. If the original source is regained and the sense of separation is put to an end, then there is peace.

Consider what happens when a stone is thrown up. It leaves its source, is projected up, tries to come down, and is always in motion until it regains its source where it is at rest. Similarly the waters of the ocean evaporate, form clouds that are moved by winds, condense into water, and falls as rain. The water rolls down the hill in streams and rivers until it reaches its original source, the ocean. After reaching there it is at peace.

So you see where there is a sense of separateness from the source there is agitation and movement until the sense of separateness is lost. So it is with yourself. Now that you identify yourself with the body, you think that you are separate. Before this false identity ceases, you must regain your source, then you can be happy.

Gold is not an ornament but the ornament is nothing but gold. Whatever shape the ornament may assume and however different the shapes of the ornaments are, there is only one reality, which is gold. Similarly with the bodies and the Self, the Reality is the Self. To identify ourselves with the body and to seek happiness is like attempting to ford a lake on the back of an alligator. The body identity is due to extroversion and the wandering of the mind. To continue in that state will only keep one in an endless tangle and there will be no peace. Seek your source, merge in the Self and remain as one.

Rebirth really means discontent with the present state and a desire to be born where there will be no discontent. Birth, being of the body, cannot affect the Self. The Self remains ever, even after the body perishes. The discontent is due to the wrong identity of the eternal Self with the perishable body. The body is a necessary adjunct of the ego. If the ego is killed, the eternal Self is revealed in all Its glory. . . .

A wise man crushes the ego at its source. It rises again and again, for him as well as for the ignorant, impelled by nature, which is *prārabdha*. Both in the ignorant and the wise the ego sprouts up, but with this difference; the former ego is quite ignorant of its source, or is not aware of its deep sleep in the dream and wakeful states. On the contrary, a wise man enjoys his transcendental experience with this ego, keeping his attention *(lakṣya)* always on its source. His ego is not dangerous; it is only the ash-skeleton of a burnt rope. Even though it possesses a form; it is ineffective. By constantly keeping our focus on our source, our ego is dissolved.

The Nature of the Ego

Q: How is realization made possible?

A: There is the absolute Self from which a spark proceeds as from fire. The spark is called ego. In the case of the ignorant it identifies itself with some object simultaneously with its rise. It cannot remain independent of such association. This association is ignorance whose destruction is the object of our efforts. If ego's objectifying tendency is filled, it remains pure and merges in its source. We can separate ourselves from that which is external but not from that which is one with us. Therefore, ego is not one with the body. This must be realized in the waking state.

The quest of "Who am I" is the axe to cut off the ego. The intellect always seeks to have external knowledge, leaving knowledge of its own origin. The mind is only the identity of the Self with the body. It is a false ego that is created; it creates false phenomena in its turn, and appears to move in them. If the false identity vanishes, the Reality becomes apparent. This does not mean that Reality is not even now. It is always there and eternally the same.

Q: How to get rid of egoism?

A: If you see what the ego really is, that is enough to get rid of it. It is the ego that makes efforts to get rid of itself, so how can it die? If ego is to go, then something else must slay it. Will it ever consent to commit suicide? So first realize what is the true nature of the ego and it will go of its own accord. Examine the nature of the ego. That is the process of realization. If one sees what one's real nature is, then one will get rid of ego. Until then our efforts are just like chasing our own shadow; the more we advance, the more distant is the shadow. If we leave our own Self, then the ego will manifest itself. If we seek our true nature, then ego dies. If we are in our own Reality, then we need not trouble about the ego.

Seek your source. Find out from where the thought of "I" springs. What object can we be surer of and know more certainly than our Self? This is direct experience and cannot further be described. If the present "I" goes, it, the mind, is known for what it is—a myth. What remains is the pure Self. In deep sleep the Self exists without perception of body and world, then happiness reigns.

Q: You say that we shall find the divine center inside us. If each individual has a center are there then millions of divine centers?

A: There is only one Center to which there is no circumference. Dive deep within and find It. Meditating on Him or on the Seer, the Self, there is a mental vibration "I" to which all are reduced. Tracing the source of "I," the primal "I" alone remains, and It is inexpressible.

Q: Is there not an unchanging Self and a changing self?

A: Changefulness is mere thought. All thoughts rise after the arising of the "I-thought." See to whom these thoughts arise. Then you transcend them and they subside. That is to say, tracing the source of the "I-thought," you realize the perfect "I". "I" is the name of the Self. . . .

Seek the True Self

Q: Is it possible to know the after-death state of a person?

A: It is possible, but why try to know it?

Q: Because I consider my son's death to be real from my level of understanding.

A: The birth of the "I-thought" is the son's birth; its death is the person's death. After the "I-thought" has arisen, the wrong identity with the body arises. Thinking yourself as the body, you give false values to others and identify them with bodies. Did you think of your son before his birth? Only as you are thinking of him, he is your son. Where has he gone? He has gone to the source from which he sprang. He is one with you. As long as you are, he is there too.

See the real Self and this confusion with the body will vanish. You are eternal, and others will be found to be eternal. Until this truth is realized there will always be this grief due to wrong identity. Birth, death, and rebirth should only make you investigate the question and find out that there are no births or rebirths; they relate to the body and not to the Self.

Q: What happens to the created ego after the body dies?

A: Ego is "I-thought." In its subtle form, it remains a thought whereas in its gross aspect, it embraces mind, senses, and body. They disappear in deep slumber along with the ego. Still the Self is there. Similarly it will be in death. Ego is not an entity independent of the Self in order that it might be created or destroyed by itself. It functions as an instrument of the Self and periodically ceases to function, that is, it appears and disappears as birth and death.

Q: I want to find the real "I" and always be effortlessly in touch.

A: It is enough that you give up the individual "I" and no effort will be needed to gain the real "I." Do not think that there is any such difference between you and the Self; then surrender yourself to Him, merge yourself in Him. There should be no reservations, as you cannot cheat God.

Q: What about after death?

A: Inquire first who or what it is that is born. It is the body, not you. Why trouble about things beyond you such as death when your Self is here and present?

Q: How long does one stay in other worlds between births and deaths?

A: The sense of time is relative. In a dream you may live a whole day's events in a couple of hours. In the subtle body of the death world you may do the same and live like what seems a thousand years, although by our time it may be only a hundred years.

Do we fear sleep? Sleep is temporary death. Death is longer sleep. Why should you want continuance of the bodily shackles? Find out your undying Self and be immortal.

As long as you identify yourself with the gross body, thoughts materialized as gross manifestations must be real to you. Having existed here it certainly survives death. Hence under these circumstances the other world exists. On the other hand, consider that the one reality is the Self from whom has sprung the ego. The ego loses sight of the Self and identifies it-self with the body, which results in ignorance and misery. The life-current [the Self] has passed through innumerable incarnations, births, and deaths, but is still unaffected. There is no reason to mourn. The mind is of the ego, and the ego rises from the Self.

The sacred bull (Nandi) in India represents the ego, *jīva*. It is always shown in our temples facing God with a flat circular stone in front of it. This stone altar is where sacrifices are offered and it all symbolizes that the ego must be sacrificed and must be turned toward the inner God.

XIV

Dying to the Little Self

by *Swami Chidananda*

There is a very significant saying: "Be still and know that I am God." When the human consciousness is constantly saying, "I am, I am, I am this, I am that," it does not provide an opportunity for the reception of the constant signal from within of the cosmic Being which whispers: "I am, I am, eternally I am. I exist, I am the Reality, I am the Truth, I am the one Being, I am your highest good, I am your supreme Glory, I am your ultimate destiny." This is not heard because of the little "I am, I am, I am," and its constant unbroken note.

Therefore, the great illumined and enlightened sages and seers evolved a method of gradually silencing this little "I am" by transcending it through thinking of others, through the sublime giving of oneself for the joy to others, for the benefit of others. By giving of oneself for the good of others, one creates a counter-situation where one has no time to listen to the constant clamor of this little "I am." By understanding the rationale and purpose behind this method and thus transcending oneself, focusing one's attention upon something other than the self, the self is gradually and ultimately weaned out of its puerile habit of "I am, I am, I am" which is spiritual childishness, a spiritual aberration, spiritual infancy, and an infantile manifestation.

This spiritually infantile, constant affirmation of the little "I" is very wisely transcended by bringing the focus of the inner being (*antahkarana*) upon sublime giving of oneself (*dāna*); sublime sacrifice (*yajña*) and sublime *tapas*—the restraining of the constant manifestation and vehement affirmation of the human consciousness represented by this "I" personality.

Thus, when the attention of the inner being is gradually diverted toward noble things other than the self, several things are achieved simultaneously. The affirmation of the "I," the little self, gradually ceases its hold upon consciousness. The human consciousness gradually becomes refined, it is thinned out and on its way to being eliminated. That is what selfless service; service of mother and father, service of society, service of the guru, service of God in the form of the poor, and compassion to creatures does. Consciousness is now being liberated from the constant nagging harassment of the little self.

This process is initiated and set going by shifting the consciousness from being I-centered to being we-centered, you-centered, all-centered to the concern of all. You think of the welfare of every creature you encounter in life, be it an ant, a spider, a plant, a flower, a leaf, or any creature, bird, or beast. All human beings become your concern and your human nature is ennobled, and uplifted.

Now, at this stage, a second phase of this liberating oneself from human consciousness is brought into being. A great love is created for the Divine, for the Reality. Self-love becomes God-love. Self-love is subdued and overcome first by compassion toward all creatures, and then it becomes diverted toward the divine, Godward.

An intensification of this process marks the third phase, when the mind is withdrawn not only from the external world of multifarious objects, but it is also withdrawn from itself. One empties oneself of oneself, and the attention is withdrawn from all the numerous nuances that go to represent this barrier, this screen, this thing which holds you back from attaining the supernal consciousness of the God which is "You," the God which is the inner real identity, the real "I AM," the great "I AM." And thus this wonderful process of unfoldment moves on.

Die to Live

The culmination of the process is what Guru Maharaj [Swami Sivananda] has summed up as, "Die to live, lead the Divine Life." "When shall I be free? When I shall cease to be, then shall I be free." Then shall be the great orb, the great sunrise of God-awareness, God-consciousness, the great day of days, of rejoicing, of hallelujah, of victory. And this human consciousness is set to rest forever. There will be a total complete absence of the false "I." "For it is in dying to the little self that one attains to everlasting life." It does not mean some grand or imaginary, fanciful, postmortem stage or other-worldly stage. Everlasting life is here and now and dying to the little self is the process of yoga.

This "dying to the little self" of St. Francis and those words of Gurudev are all built into these spiritual processes called *niṣkāma karma yoga*, and *bhakti yoga*, where the individual has no time to think of himself. All thought is upon the beloved, upon the Lord, upon the universal Being. It proceeds to an oblivion of the little self by constant focusing upon the Supreme Reality, meditation.

Meditation does not necessarily mean sitting with closed eyes in some corner in the lotus position. Meditation is a state of mind. When it is God that holds the field, God that pulls the attention, when the focusing is not on the self and its various manifestations, but on the Overself; that state of mind is called meditation. It is this constant state of meditativeness, God-centeredness, that ultimately brings about God-consciousness.

It is the world that gives us the opportunity to come out of the cocoon, the net, the prison house of I-life where "I" is the constant subject of concern. The world has been put there to help us evolve from this morbid metaphysics and to gradually expand the consciousness. And to this end, having recognized that we live in a friendly world where everything, every object, every situation, everything that surrounds us, is there to help us in this process of evolution, we have to also recognize the necessity of similarly making our interior a friendly world, a friendly inner universe where everything is helping us toward this supreme glorious consummation.

As long as this inner universe has not also been converted into a benign, friendly environment, you will be opposing yourself, delaying that great day, that wonderful day. *Śubha saṁskāras* (auspicious, good mental impressions) have to be invoked. Auspicious desires are to be encouraged, cultivated, strengthened, activated, and constantly indulged in. Harmony is to be made to prevail in every way. And the further the "I" recedes away from the horizon of our inner vision and awareness, the more friendly becomes the inner environment for our self-unfoldment.

Then we bring paradise. We live in a friendly outer world, we live in a friendly inner world. Nature (*prakṛti*) becomes our real mother and our *antaḥkaraṇa* (inner being) becomes our real best friend. It becomes our greatest asset, our supreme help in transcending the human consciousness and emerging into the glorious state of divine Consciousness, God-consciousness which is our reality, which in truth we ever are (*jīva* is verily *Brahman*).

May we thus have the discipline and learn the skill, the know-how, of this all-important process of making for ourselves a friendly world in both the exterior and the interior. *Prakṛti* immediately becomes a friend of those who are befriended by God. The Lord befriends those who give themselves to Him, befriend Him, want Him, and think of Him. Lord Krishna says: "Always, place your mind upon Me, your intellect upon Me, become Mine, salute Me, then I give you everything that is worthwhile."

Thus, if God becomes our supreme value, we are constantly dwelling in Him, then He befriends us and *prakṛti* becomes our greatest friend. Then our own interior, through the grace of God, also transforms itself into an environment conducive to our highest welfare.

Pronunciation of Sanskrit Letters

a (b*u*t)	k (s*k*ate)	ḍ ⎫ no	m (*m*uch)
ā (mom)	kh(*K*ate)	ḍh ⎬ English	y (*y*oung)
i (*i*t)	g (*g*ate)	ṇ ⎭ equiva-	r (d*r*ama)
ī (b*ee*t)	gh(*g*awk)	lent	l (*l*uck)
u (s*u*ture)	ṅ (si*ng*)	t (*t*ell)	v (*w*ile/*v*ile)
ū (p*oo*l)	c (*ch*unk)	th (*t*ime)	s (*sh*ove)
ṛ (*r*ig)	ch(mat*ch*)	d (*d*uck)	ṣ (bu*sh*el)
ṝ (*rrr*ig)	j (*J*ohn)	dh (*d*umb)	s (*s*o)
ḷ no	jh (*j*am)	n (*n*umb)	h (*h*um)
English	ñ (bu*n*ch)	p (s*p*in)	ṁ (nasaliza-
equiva-	ṭ ⎫ no	ph (*p*in)	tion of
lent	ṭh ⎬ English	b (*b*un)	preceding
e (pl*a*y)	⎭ equiva-	bh (ru*b*)	vowel)
ai (h*i*gh)	lent		ḥ (aspira-
o (t*o*e)			tion of
au(c*o*w)			preceding
			vowel)

MANANAM BACK ISSUES
(continued from page ii)

For information contact:
Chinmaya Mission West
P.O. Box 129
Piercy, CA 95587
(707) 247-3488